VERMONT COLLEGE
MONTPELIER, VT.

about 5:00. was
academic Dec. 8

Ralph Adams Brown Sp.(T)½c

S"a"- Prep - Inst.
USCG- Groton, Conn.
29 November, 1944.

MANY A
WATCHFUL NIGHT

Books by John Mason Brown

MANY A WATCHFUL NIGHT

✳

TO ALL HANDS—AN AMPHIBIOUS ADVENTURE

✳

INSIDES OUT

✳

ACCUSTOMED AS I AM

✳

BROADWAY IN REVIEW

✳

TWO ON THE AISLE

✳

THE ART OF PLAYGOING

✳

THE MODERN THEATRE IN REVOLT

✳

UPSTAGE

✳

LETTERS FROM GREENROOM GHOSTS

✳

THE AMERICAN THEATRE (1752-1934)
AS SEEN BY ITS CRITICS

(edited with Montrose J. Moses)

✳

Off Normandy

Rear Admiral (now Vice Admiral) Alan G. Kirk, USN
Watches the Invasion's Progress

LT. JOHN MASON BROWN, USNR

MANY A WATCHFUL NIGHT

Golden care!
That keep'st the ports of slumber open wide
To many a watchful night!

KING HENRY IV, PART II

WHITTLESEY HOUSE

New York McGraw-Hill Book Company *London*

MANY A WATCHFUL NIGHT

Copyright, 1944, by the McGraw-Hill Book Company, Inc.

This book is produced in full compliance with the government's regulations for conserving paper and other essential materials.

PUBLISHED BY WHITTLESEY HOUSE
A division of the McGraw-Hill Book Company, Inc.

Printed in the United States of America

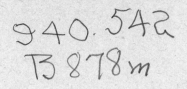
To
CASSIE,
PRESTON AND MEREDITH
and
ALL OTHER FAMILIES
ALSO A PART OF
THE INVASION

Contents

I. OVERTURE

II. BACKGROUNDS

III. ACTION

I
Overture

"But the waiting time, my brothers,
Is the hardest time of all."
Sarah Doudney, *Psalms of Life*

Chapter I

The Shadows Before

We were watching the skies with an interest unknown to men reared in peaceful cities, where weather is a week-end worry. We were watching the gray skies, and the gray, choppy, rain-speckled waves around us.

No. This is wrong. This past tense is a lie. It is history's prerogative when the fears and hopes of men, materialized as deeds, have cooled into those facts which other people read with interest or with boredom.

Participants have their own whittled sense of time. They do not know, they cannot guess, the story's outcome. They are un certain about the minute's end. Battles are not faced or fought in the past tense. Men going into battle admit only one tense— the present. A suspensive present it is, cut off, except in sudden flashes of memory, from what has been and with the future quiveringly unrevealed. So, for truth's sake, let's start out all over again.

We *are* glancing intently at those choppy waves, each one of which is grayer than the battleship gray of the *Augusta* on which we stand or of the ships huddled near us within the harbor. We *are* scanning the heavy English clouds above us, not thinking for the moment of enemy planes or of what soft pillows they would find here.

It is Monday, June 5; the afternoon of the second day we have waited. *We* have waited? The whole world has been waiting. For slow months and slowly quickening weeks, all the nations

3

and all the separated families belonging to those nations have been waiting. They have been waiting with rumors rising tidally; with the faraway wiseacres speaking knowledgeably about what they cannot know, about what only the anxious few do know.

This waiting is not easy for anyone. If anything it must be harder for those hung upon their radios at home with nothing to do except to listen from a fearful distance; to listen and read, remember and dread. It is not easy even for us lucky ones who are present, who have been trained in time-filling duties, and hence can find that blessed release from apprehension which is action.

On the Sunday that was yesterday we had thought the Invasion would start. We trust it will today. We are only the men crowded on one cruiser in one crowded harbor's worth of the armada scheduled to sail. In port after port along England's southern coast, in ports in Wales, in ports to the north in Scotland and in Ireland, other vessels, large and small, freighted with arms and men, with history and with hopes, are waiting, more tightly clustered than the grapes of wrath.

Yesterday we waited through the long Sabbath stretches. Yesterday we waited through the nervous watches of that Sunday night when *they* might have come—when in fact *they* should have come—over. Today we have waited restlessly through the routines of this fateful Monday.

Each waiting ship is a "sealed" ship, carrying men too much in the know to touch any shore now but the far shore. We have heard it whispered that there is only a three-day interval so blessed by the moon and the tides that the Invasion could at present start. In other words, we have heard it said that if it does not take place now, it could not—would not—happen until another two weeks of spiritual quarantine have snailed past, and the tides and the moon are our allies once again.

Yesterday most of us had gone to church. Men begin going to church as battles draw near. D-day is a more potent revivalist than Moody, Billy Sunday, or the McPherson who was Aimee Semple. Men begin going to church in droves. The toughest

4

O God, Our Help in Ages Past

sailors; the guys whose speech is as a rule proudly, patently un-influenced by the liturgy, they all begin going to church, even if they haven't bent an elbow to lift a hymnal in months.

Church services yesterday had not been held in the open air of the *Augusta*'s well deck. It was on the well deck some weeks previously, with the men trimly lined up, that the *Augusta* had paid its official respects as flagship of the American Task Forces to Secretary Knox.

Admiral Kirk had spoken at those simple services, pointing out how in democratic America the Navy had always been in civilian hands since the Republic's founding, and how capable were Mr. Knox's hands. Admiral Deyo, a close friend of the Secretary, had spoken of him affectionately in those sparse, precise, doubly moving words of the sea-trained. And taps, for a man and a sym-bol, dead thousands of miles away back home in the nation's capital, had been sounded by two bugles, so placed on that clean spread of steel which is a cruiser that the echoes came back from the foremast as gently as if they were floating down the hills of Arlington.

Yesterday, though the sun had crept out to reconnoiter for a few deceptive minutes, the church services were held in the hot confines of the forward Mess Hall. Captains, messboys, petty officers, yeomen, gunners, marines, cooks, junior officers, and sol-diers—we had all come unordered to this service which we sus-pected of being the last one—well, the last one before the Inva-sion. We had all come, or almost all, including the fellows who seem incapable of avoiding in every sentence a certain blunt, four-letter word which serves as a whole dictionary, since they are given to using it as noun, adjective, or verb, and using it abusively as if it had no association with pleasure.

They were all there yesterday, facing on the improvised altar a red triptych in which two angels, serene in spite of having been drafted, went calmly about their war jobs, the one employing his, her, or its Botticelli fingers to support a bomber, the other a de-stroyer. The hymns were properly amphibious—"For Those in Peril on the Sea," "Onward, Christian Soldiers," and "O God,

6

Our Help in Ages Past." They were those sturdy standbys in which, comfortably familiar as they are, men keep rediscovering new meanings when danger rewrites them.

On the front page of the typed leaflet handed to each man, the young Chaplain, Lieutenant (jg) R. G. Gordon, had printed from the eighth verse of the 121st Psalm words radiant with reassurance, "The Lord shall preserve thy going out and thy coming in from this time forth, and even for evermore."

On the same leaflet, under the heading of "Our Purpose," he had also quoted from the Atlantic Charter the article which reads, "To destroy Nazi tyranny and establish a peace which will afford to all nations the means of dwelling in safety within their own boundaries, and which will afford insurance that all the men in all the lands may live out their lives in freedom from fear and want."

All of us, I think, gathered in that hot messroom and further warmed by the emotion stirred there, had been grateful for the happy appropriateness of being reminded just then of these words. Each confused man on every crowded ship needed to be prodded into remembrance of the reason for the ordeal about to come. Needed to be prodded? More accurately, wanted to be prodded. Unless men have the minds and souls of Hessians, there is strength for them no less than consolation in knowing the whys of death, danger, and destruction.

We, you see, we felt we owned the Atlantic Charter just a little more than most mortals could claim to do, inasmuch as it was on the *Augusta* that the charter had been written.

It was the *Augusta* which had carried Mr. Roosevelt north—with Fala—to the cool waters of Argentia Bay during those hot August days of 1940, when Mr. Churchill had journeyed on the *Prince of Wales* to meet him there. The President had slept and worked in the cabin now occupied by Admiral Kirk. He and the Prime Minister had conferred under an awning stretched across the big guns of our forward turret.

That meeting had sent out the *Augusta*, four years later, once again history-bound. That meeting was one of our reasons, no

7

less than hers, for finding ourselves where we were; waiting; waiting impatiently in a harbor from which the Pilgrims, also interested in certain of those Four Freedoms, had set forth long ago.

It is not often that in its stage settings history so neatly shares Sardou's sense of theatre. It is not often that simple men, without the power of selection, discover two fat slices of history heaped on their plates like double portions of watermelon. None of us was unaware of the felicity of that coincidence which found the Atlantic Charter's mothership the flagship of America's Task Forces Invasion-bound.

This Sunday morning had passed. We had remained at anchor. The exultation had ebbed away of that church service during which many tough, gruff guys had bowed their heads for Communion in the ageless posture of acceptance as simply—and, for the moment, as innocently—as if they were children kneeling by their cribs at night. Thereafter, our restlessness had risen. The good old four-letter words had come back quickly into currency. Yesterday we had continued looking at those choppy gray waves, and grayer skies, even as we are looking at them now.

The hush of impending events was still upon us. In our hearts we felt it. At luncheon—a regular luncheon—we had tried to talk just as if it were any meal. There were jokes and silences, often both of them bad. As the afternoon crawled by, we watched with naked curiosity the stream of conferees on their way into or from Admiral Kirk's cabin; the cabin of our Chief of Staff, Admiral Struble; and Captain Jones's cabin now occupied by General Bradley.

We gaped with equal interest as the Gold Braid was piped aboard or leaving. We saw the long outlines of a column of ships silhouetted against the horizon, like clay ducks moving slowly in a shooting gallery. We noted joyfully that they were headed outward into the Channel. Our ears were cocked for the raising of the hook or for a whisper from the engineer.

We haunted the crowded Joint Operations Room set up in the hangar astern of the well deck. We collected our K-ration boxes

Waiting

for the long hours ahead when the stoves in the galleys would be cold and the messboys at their Battle Stations either manning the 20-millimeter guns midships or serving as stretcher bearers. When we met old friends, or new, in groups of twos or threes, we talked about what *It* might be like, about our chances, and without embarrassment about our families.

By the late afternoon of this endless Sunday, we had learned that *It* was off for a day. Dinner advertised the fact that *It* had been scheduled for this Sunday. Dinner consisted of mounds of turkey and ice cream and all those Leonardo da Vinci trimmings with which the Navy, in Sing Sing's most benevolent manner, prepares the stomach for the end.

After chow when prowling in the long English twilight from bow to fantail, I had heard singing in the same forward Mess Hall which had served as a church that morning. Stumbling down a ladder, I found assembled in the sweaty darkness there some thirty sailors and marines gathered around a piano. Sailors and marines? Kids in uniform, really. And what were they singing? "Praise the Lord and Pass the Ammunition"; "When Irish Eyes Are Smiling"; "For Me and My Gal"; "Deep in the Heart of Texas"; and, yes, "Auld Lang Syne." The usual, the inevitable songs, you might say, for men of good will with nonoperatic voices but with plenty of homesickness and muffled fears. So these songs were, but their sentimentality was endowed with overtones undreamed of by their composers.

"Christ! Mr. Brown," said one marine to me. "A night like this makes you think of the folks back home, don't it?"

Is that sentimentality? Is that hokum? War is the open season for both. Its hokum—its deliberate hokum—can be among the most appalling of its horrors. But its honest sentimentalities are different. Only the too comfortable, the too protected, the unterrified, the unimaginative, or the entirely untouched confuse the two, or misjudge, and are embarrassed by, these sentimentalities when they speak not from device or for effect but from human need.

10

Farewell to England

War's habit—indeed, its business—is to hit below the belt. Its savageries have no connection with sophistication. Its processes are too irrational to permit the reason to indulge in those nice distinctions between sentiment and sentimentality which are critically among the peacetime pleasures.

Hourly, war fires the ack-ack of its anguishes against the most primary emotions. The enormity of its bad taste cannot be expected to produce a flowering of good taste. No guns speak reticently. The emotional responses of war are as simple as its weapons are complicated. It reduces the complexities of the heart to a few essentials as surely as it dwindles the paraphernalia of living into the contents of a rucksack. One of the few decent things about war's indecencies is that they compel men to speak openly, unashamedly, about what is foremost in their hearts.

That marine was right. He spoke everyone's truth, even though most of us had struggled to keep it back. An evening such as yesterday's does carry the thoughts homeward with a gulpy vengeance.

If today the less scientific ones among us feel better as we are watching those gray skies and choppy waves, it's because of something that happened, something we saw last night. I don't mean Alfred Hitchcock's *Lifeboat,* which with hilarious inappropriateness was flashed as our final movie on the screen in the Junior Officers' Wardroom. I mean something we saw in the sky.

We saw it when our hearts were at their heaviest with wondering and impatience, and when the slight rain had ceased for a moment. It was then that, rising off our stern from the wet green-checkered fields of England to arch in the gray skies above us straight across the Channel to France, there had appeared the most luminous rainbow any of us had ever seen. For ten minutes it had shone, tropical in its colors. Those of us who had seen it smiled as we looked upon it, our hearts lifting. Perhaps, at such a moment we won't be blamed for having seized upon this rainbow as an omen—as the best of all possible omens in a world most decidedly not Dr. Pangloss's.

12

In the dark stretches of last night a few of us had heard that Admiral Kirk and General Bradley had gone for long conferences ashore. We could only guess at what decisions General Eisenhower and the Supreme Command had reached, and either stand our watches or snatch some sleep on cots in the overcrowded passageways or cabins, before the days and nights without rest would be upon us.

This morning at breakfast, when no ship's newspaper had appeared, we had continued to discuss the infuriating item we had read in yesterday's mimeographed newssheet on the *Augusta*. I mean the item saying that one of the wire services had come close to imperiling us all by flashing prematurely to America word that General Eisenhower's troops had landed in France. No wire service was named in the dispatch. The story about the girl typing such a headline—just for practice—had not yet appeared. All of us, including the correspondents aboard, wanted the neck of the sender of that message.

This same morning from the Admiral's bridge we had watched the convoy which had set out into the Channel the night before heading home unwillingly. During the morning a tale was whispered about it that froze the blood. It told how, when all the other vessels moving early at different speeds had been notified of the postponement and, on receiving the signal, had turned back, this one mixed convoy, owing to an error, persisted on its way. Indeed, scuttlebutt whispered that this convoy had headed some twenty miles into the Channel and straight for France before the puffing destroyers sent out to overtake it had been able to reach it and shepherd it back before it gave the plan away.

At lunch time the skies were again gray and the seas choppy. They continued so during the early afternoon when we, in our uncertainty, kept scanning them for an answer as to whether or not we might be moving tonight. They are gray now, when every time we cross the well deck or go topsides we are still looking at them.

Then suddenly the word reaches us, the word which neither

the clouds nor the seas have revealed. Someone whispers it to someone who whispers it to someone else. It spreads epidemically throughout the ship. We are going. The Invasion is on. We will not have another twenty-four hours of desperate waiting. We will be spared those dreaded two weeks of confinement, waiting for the tides and moon to be with us once again. We will get under way this afternoon.

At 2:30 we hear the rumble of the anchor being raised. Soon thereafter we begin to move. So do the ships near us. We slip out into the grayness. The green fields disappear. Silent people line the shore. They have seen their harbor emptied and re-filled so many times in the preceding months that we wonder if they realize this is the real thing. A few of them wave. Not many. More impressive than these gestures of farewell is the fitting silence of the Britishers' curiosity. We understand and share this.

Before long we are out in the Channel, skirting eastward along the English coast for our first rendezvous—this time with our own forces. Our rendezvous with the enemy is scheduled for dawn tomorrow.

As soon as the night's steak and the second of our Last Suppers is downed, I climb up with my hurriedly written script to the pilot house to the fore of the Admiral's bridge to broadcast the detailed plan of the Invasion.

"Are you going to give us the hot dope tonight?" asks a gunner.

"Are you going to spill the beans tonight, Mr. Brown?" asks the chief on the signal bridge.

The pilot house is crowded with youngsters who have sensed that the moment has come for them all to be in the know.

One of my duties, you see, is to deliver to the ship's company, especially to the men below decks who in an action cannot see what is going on, the same kind of blow-by-blow description over the Public Address system which Admiral Kirk had ordered me to deliver during the Sicilian invasion.

I must admit my heart pounds this afternoon when I fasten the

14

Raising the *Augusta*'s Hook

speaker around my neck, turn the button down, and get ready to begin. I can hardly hear my own first words.

May I have your attention? Your undivided attention?

I could not have more serious things to say to you on matters more demanding of your most earnest listening.

It is here. It has come. It has come at last.

After all these months of rigorous training, after all these weary months of waiting, after all the tedium of inaction, after all these preliminary exercises and maneuvers, after the long exhausting vigils of planning, after the last-minute threats of bad weather, and yesterday's postponement, the Invasion has begun. We are on the move and so is history.

I ask you to listen attentively this afternoon not only because the plans sketched here are your life and death concern. That should be reason enough. But we, as individuals, however important we do remain to ourselves, we have just now taken on a mass significance which cannot be overestimated and beside which all of us considered singly count as nothing.

The whole wide waiting world hangs upon what will be the outcome of these next few days and nights—the whole wide waiting world and history. The future of the world—its hopes, its decencies, its dreams of freedom, of peace and of order—all these depend, no less than the future of our country, upon what these days and nights bring forth. For this is one of those moments when history holds its breath.

Because you are sailing into history is no reason for your sailing into the dark. As Admiral Kirk sees it, it is all the more reason for your setting forth in the light, with the knowledge of what you are a part of as another source of your democratic strength.

In the simplest of possible terms, let me try to lay before you the essentials of an extremely intricate and vast plan.

First of all, our objective.

We are headed for France, as you have guessed. To be specific, we are headed for the beaches in the Bay of the Seine, immediately to the east of the Cherbourg peninsula.

16

"We are headed for the beaches in the Bay of the Seine"

MANY A WATCHFUL NIGHT

We are the Western or American Task Force. To the east of us in this same area will be the Eastern or British Task Force.

If ours is, as indeed it is, history's largest combined operation, it is because in England we and the British have learned to respect one another the hard way—by being together, by laughter, by perplexity, by irritation, by the need and desire to work together. They have seen us swarm across their cities and fields in numbers comforting but uncomfortable. We, uprooted, have had to readjust ourselves to a new mode of life in an old country new to us. . . . We. . . .

II

Backgrounds

"Now all the youth of England are on fire,
And silken dalliance in the wardrobe lies:
Now thrive the armourers, and honour's thought
Reigns solely in the breast of every man:
They sell the pasture now to buy the horse, . . .
For now sits Expectation in the air."

Henry V

The Fruits of Our Factories

Chapter II

Strong to Save

When we followed Admiral Kirk to England this winter, we suspected it was the Invasion which was bringing our Task Force there. We thought we knew this, and we knew we hoped this to be true. We had had our first taste of amphibious warfare off Scoglitti in Sicily the summer before. We were aware that this experience, which had welded us as a group as only battle can, was in the nature of a preface. Now we were anxious to be in on the writing of the climactic chapters. Furthermore, we had returned from the Mediterranean to THAT TOWN. And THAT TOWN is perhaps the world's ideal port of embarkation, since anyone who has ever been based there is apt to be willing to go anywhere else.

Of course, we lesser fry did not know where or when we would strike the Continent. Still we were confident, as we packed our bags and said our good-byes in New York, that strike it we would. This helped. Because one of the greatest of service griefs is to be nonoperational and in uniform. It's like being all dressed up for football and then being asked to play on a goalless field.

What some of us failed to realize was that before *the* Invasion could take place another invasion would have to occur; in other words, that to invade Europe we would have to invade England first. Certainly when we set out in November and early December, we no more guessed than most of the British people could have done how large-scaled both of these operations were bound to be.

The leaving is never easy. In peacetime for the Regulars— maybe. In wartime—no, not even for them. There is no such thing either for the goer or for the goee as growing accustomed to say-

21

ing a farewell when the chances are that it will not be an au revoir.

In wartime any station platform skywrites this. So does any restaurant. You do not have to know the couple opposite you to know their story. Their eyes, the corners of their mouths, their very postures confess everything. One glance will tell you whether the man and woman sitting there are dining because their maid is out or because their lives are out of joint.

If the man is in uniform, and they are eating together knowing they will eat together again and again, tomorrow, the next day, and for weeks thereafter, they make this plain. Their relaxation means their meal is no more than part of a routine, and as such taken for granted. Their meetings still belong to the world of normal expectancies, of anticipated sequences. They don't have to press their fingers together to stop the running sands.

But have they re-met, after what might have been? Their eyes and faces, full of radiance, their laughter, the energy with which they overcrowd each snatched minute, even their slight uncertainty with one another—all these are the narrators of their good fortune.

Or are they on the brink of being parted? Their faces, so different now, reveal this; their eyes and the taut desperation of their bodies. This man and woman are drinking from a cup which seems empty not because it is empty but because they know it may soon be so.

They won't say this. They should not say this. They must not say it. Yet at this moment of cleavage, which masquerades so feebly as a feast, they feel, no matter how courageous they may be, that life for them has proved no more than a relentless auctioneer who, with hammer upraised, cries, "Going, going, gone!" and cries it unstoppably.

"Happy families are all alike; every unhappy family is unhappy in its own way." That was the generalization with which Tolstoy plunged into the peacetime domestic misadventures of *Anna Karenina*. He could not have employed it in *War and Peace*. There it would have been a lie, because all families included in a war know much the same unhappiness, compounded strangely as it is with pride, and suffer from identical worries.

Orders are nothing if not peremptory. *You will proceed and report to the Commandant of Such-and-Such a Naval District for temporary additional duty awaiting first available transportation, including air, to Europe. Upon arrival proceed and report to the Commander of So-and-So.* And, discounting a sequence of delays which prove merciful at last by rendering the agony of daily farewells ludicrous, you do proceed. Just as you wanted to; just as you will want to again when once you get going. But not now. Not at this moment. No, nor at every moment after you have reached there.

Orders never say proceed from what—except in terms of Commands. As if this Naval District or that Command were one's whole life. One's whole life it is, or may be, just then in the big sense of a nation's striving to live. But not your life—our life.

Orders never say who you are or what you are. Or whether you are young or oldish, mechanical or dreamy, legal or literary, farm-raised or city-bred, Northern or Southern, child-blessed or single, dreading to forgo what you must now surrender, or happy to escape.

Orders can't be expected to bother about such trifles. They are only the bookkeeping of duty. They speak to numbered men who have ceased to count, even to themselves, as individuals—at least, almost, and to all practical purposes, ceased to count. This is what a threatened country is all about. It is an aroused family of aroused families. So there is no credit to be had for trying to do what one can when it is in need.

Still, this doesn't make the going—each going—every going— easy. You know those orders are coming. Yet no one is ever prepared for them when they do come. Or for the immediate readjustments they command.

The Invasion, which is so many things, is also a mountain range of orders; hence of farewells, of empty places at the table, of incomplete Christmases, uncelebrated anniversaries, untaken weekends, and of changed lives here, there, and on the way over.

23

Before we can move across the Channel, we as Americans must have been moved across the narrowing Atlantic. Or out of Africa or Italy, and even, in the case of some officers, from the Pacific.

By sea and air, by air and sea, in convoys huge or small, on transports crowded to the gunwales and Navy-protected from the waiting U-boats, on heavy freighters dipping under breakers, in post-card weather or through black, wintery waters, on lumbering LST's, on tossing LCI(L)'s, on bucking D.E.'s and destroyers, on the large ships that race alone, on cruisers, battleships, and vessels loaded with explosives, by Clipper, by Export or on Army Transports, by the northern or southern air routes depending upon the season, we, and our guns; our gas, our DUKW's, and our tanks; our jeeps, our stretchers, and our files; our medicines and our medals; our camouflage and our small stores; our typewriters, our desks, and those reams and reams of paper which are the ignition, the oil, and the curse of an invasion; our bedding and most of our food; and everything we need to build our bases, to house our men in huts and offices, to repair our ships, and to equip us for the period both of final training and of final planning no less than for the attack itself and for its support—all of these must have been moved. Meanwhile, to England, to Greenland, and to Iceland; to Russia via the Murmansk run; to Africa, to Sicily, to Italy, to South and Central America; and to the Middle East, the life lines in the Atlantic must be kept open, while in the Pacific another major war is being waged and making equal demands.

Does this sound simple when catalogued in the Whitmanesque cadences with which Pare Lorentz hymned the rivers combining to make *The River?* This mass movement *is* a river, fresh water in salt; a man-made Mississippi of strength and arms, of steel and gasoline, of concrete and woolens, of foodstuffs and homesickness. Like the Mississippi, as Mr. Churchill noted, it just had to keep rolling along.

Certainly in the annals of migration this huge ferrying back to the Old World of the New World's accumulated prowess is a miracle. Don't think because it is executed by men in uniform who belong to organizations bearing such impersonal names as

Mass Migration

the Navy, the Army, the Marine Corps, the Coast Guard, the Merchant Marine, or the Air Force that it is not done by men with nicknames, passions, and personalities no less than with serial numbers.

The final uniformity—and glory—of uniforms is not their brass buttons, their colors, or their cut. It is the will they make clear on Charley's part, or Leo's, or Gus's or Rastus' to forgo for a common cause the play of wills in which their wearers once rejoiced. As a manifest and symbol of such a submission, even the depressing sameness of uniforms becomes stirring.

The will to be will-less comes hard to those knowing and relishing freedom. It is the first supreme sacrifice made by servicemen. The sacrifice commonly described as such is, like a safe return from battle, no more than the chance consequence of this initial submission which, whether its origins are elective or selective, makes so appalling the responsibilities of those who have invited it or those whose wills are for the duration substituted for the wills forsworn.

But do not worry. It is only the skin of an American that can be encased in a uniform. Our individualism is nowhere more rugged than among those truckdrivers, those young lawyers and doctors, those farm hands and soda jerkers, those schoolteachers or those mechanics, whose temporary duties are designated by identical clothes.

It is these uniformed men, no two of whom are cut from quite the same pattern, who make possible the prelude to the Invasion represented by this mass convergence upon Britain. This mass migration is achieved mainly by young men hailing from all the states, descended from all kinds of races, and speaking American with all kinds of accents. It is achieved by young men few of whom five years back ever thought they would be sailors, soldiers, fliers, marines, or Seabees. It is achieved by young men most of whom have not seen the sea before, and all of whom in peacetime congratulated themselves—with reason—as navigators and masters of logistics if they were able to get their wives, their children, their baggage, and all the nursery necessities off and on the train

26

Enter America, Smiling

carrying them away to a summer vacation.

This migration is carried out in spite of danger. It is accomplished with the guidance of men in the sea rooms of the Admiralty and the Eastern Sea Frontier. It is made possible by long lines of ships zigzagging their way for safety across perilous waters, and by strained eyes eternally watching the seas and the skies. It is brought about with the aid of smiling family photographs, with the encouragement of the elastic contours of pin-up girls, to the tunes of tin-pan alley scratched out on tired records, and the sound of Bob Hope's jokes.

It is the result of day and night shifts in our factories, of plants speedily built or speedily transformed to meet the new demands of new days and a war tempo, and in spite of strikes, profiteering, or soaring wage demands. It is the product of bonds bought, of pennies saved, of millions spent, of goods rationed, and of good will usually unrationed. It requires many, many more men and women to keep it moving than even it can move. An indispensable part of the fuel making it possible here and there is the mail from and to home which feeds its spirit. Without this spirit its best machinery would rust and refuse to operate.

Gradually this migration deposits on an already overcrowded England the fruits of our industries, the energies of our business, the sacrifices of our families. All over the island which is Britain, other islands rise from the sea—slowly, coral-wise, as if by accretion. These islands are those not-so-little Americas, which here, there, everywhere begin to change the British landscape, and sometimes even the British and American points of view.

"England," wrote Emerson in *English Traits,* a book which cannot be read often enough by those who would know how much and how little England has changed since the days of wooden ships full-sailed, "England resembles a ship in its shape; and if it were one, its best Admiral could not have worked or anchored it in a more judicious or effective position."

The Admirals and the Generals, and the stricken people of Coventry, Exeter, Plymouth, the East End, or Mayfair may not have blessed this anchorage in the period after Dunkerque when

Lt. Dwight Shepler

An Old Harbor, New Fishing Boats

England was preparing to fight on the beaches, and in the streets, if necessary, and when each night for many, many appalling nights the sky over London had released the horrors of the Blitz.

But last winter the war was changing. It was on German-held beaches that the British were now preparing to fight—the British, the Canadians, the New Zealanders, the Australians, the Danes, the Dutch, the Norwegians, the Czechs, the Free French; yes, and the Americans.

As we Americans moved in, the British had no other choice than to move over, which is no easy thing to do in your own house. Even the fact that they needed us, as they frankly said they did, did not make the moving over easier. To know the firehouse is eight or ten blocks away and equipped to come to your aid is one thing. To have the firemen swarm into your home and set up the hook and ladder in your front parlor and put the fire engine in the kitchen is quite another matter—hard on the fireman, harder on the houseowner. Yet this is what we did to make the Invasion possible. And this is what the British knew we had to do.

Chapter III

Under an English Heaven

If the British knew and admitted that they needed us, any American who thought, not twice but just plain thought, admitted and knew that we needed them. Had they not stood alone, we might not have been able to stand at all. We were both the stronger when we stood side by side.

Their island to our Air Force was a mammoth carrier. Their harbors offered bases to our Navy only a few hours away from German-held France. Their meadows and their golf links served our Army as grounds for maneuvers. Their war experience was of unpurchasable value. Their courage—civilian no less than military—when, and after, they were battered and almost beaten was as radiant an example of mass gallantry as history knows. In Mr. Churchill the will, the tenacity, the dauntless bravery of the whole people found a symbol during the dark days. It was not for the nation that he spoke. It was as the nation.

We came hungry to a land where food was scarce. And the British entertained us in their homes. We came thirsty to pubs and clubs where the liquor supply was low. And the British, though no less thirsty, did not appear to mind. The sole comment of an English girl, a Wren, when she watched a group of our Sahara-throated sailors gulp down in a single hour a village pub's liquor supply for an entire evening, was, "I say, you Americans don't seem to savor your pleasures, do you?"

The British welcomed us cheerfully, and put up no less cheerfully with the inconveniences we caused them even when they did not welcome us. We crowded their hotels. We crowded their streets. We crowded their countryside. We added to their dif-

31

ficulties in getting taxis. We depleted the meager stocks in their stores. We jammed their theatres and their restaurants, their movies and their trains.

We moved into requisitioned buildings in every bruised village, town, or city where our forces were stationed. Where there were no towns, we built them. We built them in the rubble left by air raids or in woods and meadows hitherto unscarred. We built them in the coast towns and in parks far inland. Hut camps mushroomed over England. Our relentless bulldozers broke the ground for them, plowing up dark mud where green turf had flowered for centuries, and overturning old oaks to make way for macadam roads over which our jeeps raced.

All roads and most leaves led to London. And London, while remaining an overcrowded London, had to find room for all our men in every service who, feeling life was threatened, journeyed there for a few days' respite. London also had to find room for London and the Empire. She led a multiple life under the direst difficulties. She was at once the capital of a great power and the seat of many exiled governments who then knew no other capital. She was a pleasure town and a war zone. She was the headquarters for the Invasion forces, and the nerve center of a global war straining the resources of her Dominions. She was a metropolis in her own rights, and for her own citizens, and a week-end release for men on leave every day in the week. She was a favorite enemy target, too. Meanwhile, she served the Americans who poured into her not only as an annex to Washington but as a substitute for New York.

Americans in or out of uniform, on every kind of mission, and in every branch of the service must have appeared as inexhaustible to Londoners as England's supply of Brussels sprouts did to Americans. So far as accents and uniforms were concerned, Mayfair could have been Camp Dix or Camp Bradford. In and around our headquarters square, which came to be known as Eisenhower Plàtz, English, as the English speak it, was almost a foreign language. It was as rare as a Down East twang on the campus at Tuskegee or the speech of the Canterbury Pilgrims in the House of Lords.

Middletown—Great Britain

A Quonset Hut Camp

Our service offices spilled over, little by little, into so many buildings thereabouts that even we understood the justice of the cartoon in *Punch* which showed a very dignified and bewildered couple from the provinces coming up to a bobby in Mayfair to ask, "Can you tell us where the native quarter is?"

Little effort is required to imagine how we would have felt at home, or what certain of our newspapers might have said, had the Royal Navy been granted full possession of Annapolis during a war which we, with Britain's aid, were waging against an enemy in the New World. But the British moved out, and our Navy moved into the Royal Naval College at Dartmouth without anyone's protesting.

On the south coast of Devon, in the area of Slapton Sands, by Britain's invitation, we went further. In British eyes this was a necessary part of having the Invasion succeed, of getting the war over. To them this was reason enough.

We turned our troops, our rockets, and our heaviest guns loose —and loose in earnest—on English villages and farmhouses in a triangular strip of coast from which the inhabitants had been evacuated. Our maneuvers, in which British ships participated, were more than dress rehearsals. They were full-fledged performances, carried out as earnestly as if D-day were already upon us.

People, old and young, whose families had lived for generations in the same houses, were asked, for a weekly compensation and as part of the war effort, to gather up their possessions; their pictures, their china, their furniture, their clothes, their dogs, even their goats, in cars supplied by the WVS. They moved, choking the roads with their traffic, so that their homes, serving as targets, could bear the blasting impact of our guns. Had they been the enemy, these Britishers could not have had less to return to. At the entrance to one church a minister had posted a sign asking us please to spare the parish dead in the near-by graveyard. The sign was a request, not a protest.

Then, all over England, and totally beyond the rulings of Lend-Lease, there were lonely American men—and English girls.

No. Our moving in was not easy. Either for the British who

God Save the Queen

Moving Day in the Evacuated Area

needed us or for us who needed them.

When we arrived in England, most of us, as we left our planes or ships, had our first experience with a beleaguered land. A country under attack is very different from a nation merely at war. We inhaled that difference with our first breath on British soil.

At home we remembered how, when the war was young for us, many American cities had manifested their civic pride in new ways. Men cannot bear to be too far removed from the importance of disaster. After Pearl Harbor good, zealous patriots in this city or that had convinced themselves of the enemy's special interest in their towns. It was an odd flowering of Rotary, this desire to have a town's industrial importance recognized in such a destructive way. But cities vied with one another for the doubtful honor of being more accessible than the next to Japanese or German bombers. Loyal citizens would whip out an orange and a bit of string, like veteran transatlantic passengers in peacetime, to prove that the great circle from Berlin or Tokyo led directly to their doorsteps, whether they lived far inland or on the seacoasts.

No oranges had to be consulted to know how near Bristol or Plymouth were to Berlin. And none were on hand for consultation.

Whole areas, reduced to cobblestones and as neatly raked as flower beds, told the story. So did gutted buildings, their facings gone, their floors collapsed, the location of their staircases marked by gashes on the now naked plaster of their interiors, and their fireplaces and bedroom wallpapers pathetic in the guarantee of intimacy they had once offered.

The first sight of the barriers around the arrival points told the same story. So did the first conversation with British sentries. The trains up to London were wartime trains, cold and packed, in which the window blinds were pulled down securely at night, and the lights kept low. These measures were not precautions against what might be. They were safeguards against what had been again and again, and might at any moment recur.

Repaired in England

Many Americans, coming to England in the winter months, reached London during a black-out. They emerged from trains, which now seemed blinding in their brightness, to be swallowed up in the darkness. They stepped out into a world consisting only of infinite folds of a black velvet curtain far too heavy to lift.

The lights of New York or Washington were still in their eyes. The lights of their home towns, too. The "dim-outs" in the States were noonday compared with the midnight of a moonless black-out. London, unlighted, seemed darker than the darkest country-side through which the train had passed. It seemed darker, because one of the most inviting aspects of cities should be that they do not recognize the night except to defy it and to celebrate their defiance.

There was nothing retail about the London darkness. It was depressingly wholesale. Add to this darkness, which was foglike, a real fog, a London fog, which is the realest fog there is, and you found yourself trapped and entombed by the mere absence of light.

Although some Americans learned slowly to lightning-bug their way with hooded flashlights through the black streets, and others developed sufficient night vision to stroll about as unlighted as if they were Britishers, many of us never grew accustomed to the moonless black-outs of the interminable winter nights. They were as deflating to the spirits as they were hard on locomotion. We wondered how the British, having faced them for so long, still managed to rise above them. We admired them the more because of their refusal to be discouraged or deterred.

We dreaded these winter nights between moons. We dreaded not only their coming but our going out in them. We dreaded getting up in the tar-thick darkness on cold mornings, stumbling to the office down inky streets, and wading out again into the blackness in the late afternoons. All winter long, we looked forward to the spring with its ever-lengthening twilights, its early dawns, and its deliverance from lightlessness.

The black-outs clung to certain places by day with regrettable fidelity. Their reluctance to forsake the train sheds in London

The Army Moves In

stations was always evident. "Pittsburgh," a taxi driver there had once explained to me in the early morning as an answer to a complaint about the darkness, "Pittsburgh," he had said, "is the only city that enjoys a natural black-out."

The London train sheds obviously shared an identical sense of enjoyment. No smudged and faded Whistlers could have been murkier than they contrived to be on gray days, even at lunchtime. If they rejoiced in their gloom by day, they reveled in it orgiastically by night. Then, they were tunnels of steam, soot, and smoke, leading not to light but to deeper darkness.

Most newly arrived Americans, when they had at last found their way to their hotels, after having been driven through an invisible London by drivers equipped to serve the Seeing Eye, went to bed wondering what the night would bring. The war-zone feeling was then heavily upon them, however much in the future they might lose that feeling for weeks at a time, or come to scoff at the "Battle of Headquarters Square."

In their rooms, reading in bed with the windows open was a lost pleasure. One of many. The connections with home were definitely broken. They were alone in a strange city at war, within easy reach of enemy planes. The ebony black-out curtains at their windows announced this; announced it incessantly. Although Americans soon learned to take them for granted, these curtains were always at hand, in their flats and offices, in every office, home, or public place they visited. They were never out of sight; permanent shadows on the most cheerful walls. From each sunset to each sunrise, except at the opened windows in darkened bedrooms, their bat wings were outstretched, their blackness spread the wider. They were the mourning which all threatened buildings in all threatened lands wore for peace. The crepe which draped the Strasbourg monument in the Place de la Concorde for years before the last war could not have been a more eloquent reminder of what had been lost than were these funeral hangings.

Daylight, however, was needed to have London reveal her scars. A ride in a taxi left many of these undisclosed. Only the more spectacular were then noticeable.

40

The churches, such as St. Clement Danes, roofless and charred, their windows gone; the flattened Pompeian areas near the docks in the East End or around St. Paul's; the ancient stones in the Temple, now fragments on the ground; the missing portico in Whitehall, where the Horse Guards had once sat as imperturbable as toy soldiers; the damage in Pall Mall across from St. James's Palace or to the Palace itself—these could not be missed.

They caught the eyes at once, like empty sleeves dangling from the uniforms of veterans. What had happened to them, and to countless more of their kind, were sins against history or beauty. They were the four-starred Baedeker horrors. Any overnight tourist would have been on the lookout for them.

You had to walk to realize the full extent of London's wounds. London's reticence about them was in the best British tradition as we Americans had been led to expect it. As a matter of fact, it was too much in the stage or fictional tradition to be any truer than these traditions are.

The British are reticent only when other Britishers are present. They silence one another by their shared sense of class and propriety. Leave them alone with strangers, including Americans, and they regain their speech. After a dignified interval—say, three train stations—they can be garrulity itself.

They emerge from the genteel hibernation into which they have been driven by others of their race and shed their autobiographies in the sunlight of foreigners. Each one of them is a Buchmanite at heart; each train compartment, a confessional week-end. You leave strangers, knowing more about them at a first meeting than you do about your best friend after a lifetime's confidence; that is, if no other Britishers have been on hand to make them freeze.

They take time to thaw. But once they thaw, the flood of intimacies is on. Even then, it is dignified, because Britishers are never overly familiar even with themselves. They have an enchanting way of talking about themselves as if they were other people; of using the first person singular as if it were the third.

41

This only adds to the completeness, and the surprise, of their gradual revelations.

London about her wounds was like her citizens about their lives. After a few minutes' stroll, there was no stopping her admissions. Regardless of where you turned, her sufferings were evident and slowly brought to light. They were far more extensive than was indicated even by the gutted buildings encountered in almost every block and square. Or by those entirely downed, where the basements were walled up and being used as emergency tanks for fire fighting.

These total casualties ranked among the more conspicuous scars. Right next to them were the real wounds. Avoiding notice at first, and seemingly intact, would be two, three, or five houses—sometimes an entire row—empty, their windows boarded or gone, only their walls standing, locust shells abandoned by the locusts.

By day, especially in the long winter months, London had a tired aspect. She resembled a queenly older woman who, after having suffered injuries in a bad accident, had been unable to slip into a new dress, have her hair done, or find her vanity case. She was a city wearing no make-up. She needed repainting, rebuilding; a general overhauling. But her queenliness had not been destroyed. She was proud for the proudest of fine reasons. And beautiful with that sad, tortured look of beauty which can come only to the faces of those who have suffered greatly and been capable of great suffering. What she had lost in allure, she had gained in character. There was nothing empty or cheaply pretty about her expression. Her poverty had grandeur. She wore it, as she had earned it, gallantly; like a medal. It was her highest decoration.

Moonlight was needed to restore her full beauty. Whenever it came, it performed a greater service than merely reclaiming her youth. To regain youth, and youth alone, is to rob the wise of the wisdom life has brought them. Youth is as common as experience is individual. Its sapling freshness is denied the fruits of character. Had the moonlight only made London young, it would have deprived her of those centuries during which she has ac-

42

So This Is London

cumulated the pains, the glories, the associations, the settled habits of life, the personal flowerings of taste, and the character which make her London.

The moonlight was kinder than this. Instead of salvaging her youth, it left her age unlined. It was as flattering to her as candle-light is to an older woman. If it exposed her to the enemy, it covered the scars he had inflicted on her. Its bandages were magi-cal; its healing powers supernatural. To her very wounds it brought both enchantment and mystery.

London is a city of white stones blackened and streaked by time, of pinkish-brown bricks, of open squares and gentle parks, and numberless chimney pots reaching mildly for the sky. She is a horizontal rather than a vertical city, and her spaciousness includes welcome room for vistas. She is not taut or defiant. She rests comfortably on her terrain, and on her past.

In wartime she was a stage setting waiting for the switchboard of the moonlight to do her proper justice. It washed the black streaks from her white façades until they ceased to be smudges and became the most melodramatic of shadows. It converted her parks into the kind of *décors* that made every man a balletomane.

London gave herself to the moonlight with a lover's frenzy. Under its spell she sauntered off into her past as easily as Virginia Woolf's *Orlando* had changed sex.

Although the moonlight could not hush the heavy scraping of soldiers' shoes as they echoed in London's streets, it peopled her sidewalks with the statues it had liberated from her niches and monuments. To wander under the moon's enchantment into Berkeley Square, to stand before the tracery of the Abbey to face Big Ben, to encircle St. Paul's, to walk past the Banqueting Hall, to stroll down Regent Street, to pass St. Martin's-in-the-Fields; to turn up the Mall toward the Palace, to pause on Waterloo Bridge, or to come home on the park side of Piccadilly was to know that Merlin had never died.

The London moonlight may have been cold in its snowy white-ness, but it was radiant in its intensity. It would have been wel-come for halting the black-outs even if it had not been lovely.

44

But its beauty was supernal. Only Venice was such a city for the moon as was London.

Even Americans who in the past had known London well found wartime London a new world. Bruised, facing nightly the possibility of enemy attack, her streets after dark dependent upon the moon for their brightest illumination, she was suffering from more than the abnormal disruptions and privations which are normal in time of war. She was a city both in uniform and in earnest. The war was her major concern; an ugly business requiring her full strength.

Her streets were crowded with sailors, soldiers, and airmen from each of the Allied countries, from every far-flung Dominion, and all parts of Britain, no less than from America. England's war duties were on the single standard. Women in blue, khaki, or black were as common as men, even if the architecture of their bodies often offered their uniforms a fierce and natural resistance.

Everywhere women were doing what men like to call a man's job when they mean a huge job superlatively well done. As dispatch riders on motorcycles dashing over slippery roads at all hours. With the ATS, in the WVS and the Wrens. As Navy drivers, in the factories, and on the farms. With the Red Cross or St. John's Nurses. As spotters on the roofs, on the trains and busses, at the stations, and in a thousand other capacities they were serving. One felt that England's mobilization of her adults was complete.

At first the mere size of London awed and depressed many of our young men who had been farm-raised or brought up in small towns. As country people can be, they were made lonely by the very sight of so many men and women who were strangers. London was for some of them the first great metropolis to which they had been exposed. These men took longer than their city-bred compatriots to grow accustomed to her. To them she was not only a strange city; she was a city, hence likewise strange.

But the country-reared soon learned what the city-bred had always known—that every large city is only an anthology of villages; villages to suit each taste, pocketbook, and temperament.

45

A foreign accent, a different architecture, a new diet, even a world war did not prevent London from being in this respect like every other city. To enjoy London, and forget its winter climate, one had to find the right village or, better still, the right villages.

Before we could do this, those of us on Admiral Kirk's staff had first to find our way to Number 15. This building, which housed our headquarters, was naturally the center of our London living and being.

Chapter IV

Her Ways to Roam

There were two United States Naval Commands in the same square, near neighbors at Numbers 20 and 15. There was Admiral Stark's, known as Comnaveu, because Admiral Stark was Commander of U. S. Naval Forces in Europe; and shared with the Army. And there was our Task Force, under Rear Admiral Alan G. Kirk, who was Commander of American Naval Forces participating in the Invasion.

Ours was the newcomer and the transient; Admiral Stark's the parent and more permanent organization. We, and the commands under us, were the assault group in Admiral Stark's domain, with the Invasion as our specific task. Admiral Stark's command had been in England for several years, establishing our first bases there, looking after all our naval interests in Europe, seeing that the supply lines were kept open, performing many and manifold imperative duties.

Both headquarters occupied imposing pink brick buildings, faced with white stone, and bore a family resemblance to the American Embassy. Both had been modern apartment houses. Both were so opulent in their scale, decorations, and bathroom fixtures that no one denied the story which said these apartments had been occupied by such as Marlene Dietrich or the elder Fairbanks. A few were even made the happier by this knowledge.

The two headquarters were joined by more than close ties of friendship, problems demanding joint solution, and the friendly dignity of Admiral Stark. Ultimately they were connected by a temporary bridge which reproduced in miniature that long cov-

47

ered bridge which Navy personnel must cross and recross in Washington if they would adjust their pay accounts.

In London, however, this bridge did not span a Reflecting Pool. It was suspended above a spread of rubble where, had it not been for German bombs in the days of the Blitz, a Mayfair residence would still have stood. The direct hits had come that near.

During the Blitz, hits had also been scored on the two corner mansions. Though wrecked, these remained standing, as open as dolls' houses. The battered circular staircase now leading nowhere in the one, the large paneled rooms in both, the mirrors broken above the chipped marble of exquisite fireplaces, the high ceilings pierced or fallen, and the stains on the cracked plaster where paintings had once hung, all were tragic witnesses for an elegance even now unwilling to surrender entirely. A cluster of abandoned homes on the west side of the square, which looked at first glance as habitable as those still used there, and the scars on the John Adams house on the southeast corner told of other hits.

Although these, and all of London's wounds, shocked the sensibilities of new arrivals, and shocked them profoundly, this shock —appallingly enough—diminished within a few weeks. By then we had grown as accustomed to such mutilations as modern war teaches one to be. The final comment on the times was that human eyes were so soon able, and willing, to accept such sights as normal. We began to take them as much for granted as did the Londoners who, having lived in these buildings, and then with their ruins, were no longer surprised by them. After a while, it was chiefly the new wounds which caught our attention on our way to and from our headquarters.

Every headquarters resembles the next to some extent, and all share certain features with a small principality. Each reflects the will, the tastes, and the personality of its All Highest and, because these differ, is the more like a duchy.

Since all commands, to function efficiently, must pyramid up to the Stars which shine above them, these Stars locally replace

Naked Wounds

the Sun King. Hence, whether they like it or not, every man and officer in a command is to some degree a courtier under orders.

Each headquarters, being human no less than in uniform, has its chamberlains, its privy councilors, its palace intriguers, its court jesters, its flunkies, and its gentlemen-in-waiting no less than its monarch. All headquarters know the anguishes of the ante-room and the swallowed pride of heads bowed in assent. All of them are microcosms of centralized power at work and of human nature at work under it. Each is a little kingdom with no revolutionaries permitted within its frontiers, and a business where labor disputes are unthinkable. In the Armed Services an order has to be an order. As such it must be so final and so far beyond questioning as to be a civilian executive's dream.

As a group we considered ourselves lucky in our Stars. Most of us had been with Admiral Kirk in Sicily, when he commanded one of the three task forces under Admiral Hewitt. A few of us had been with him in London the winter before the Sicilian invasion, when he had served in the joint capacity of naval attaché and Admiral Stark's Chief of Staff.

Of middle height, with twinkling blue eyes set in a sailor's weathered face, Admiral Kirk had the full confidence of his Staff. He was at once spruce and rugged, dapper and grimly determined. His walk betrayed the energy of his thinking. It was a cross between a stride and strut, which even on dry land had an uncanny way of converting a carpet into a bridge. Executed by legs which refused to forsake the sea, it was Admiral Kirk's only unamphibious aspect. His stance on land, on the rare occasions when he did stand still, found him with his hands dug thumb-deep in his blouse pockets, with his chin jutting out, and his head thrown back.

In spite of the wishbone lines which cut formidable ravines from the corners of his mouth down to the edges of his chin, his face was extremely mobile. It was quick to register his gaiety (which was genuine), his alertness (which was unflagging), his displeasure (which was authoritative), or his anger (which at those dark moments when it was released could outdo Conrad in introducing a landlubber to a typhoon).

He was a fighter, gruff, imperious, dogged, and willful, as one look at him made clear. But he was much more than that, as two minutes' conversation no less clearly demonstrated. His mind bit instantly into the heart of a subject. He was no mere sea dog in the manger. He was a suave diplomat. He knew his responsibilities as a host or guest no less than as an officer, and met them charmingly. His friendships indicated how far his interests carried him beyond the Navy's special harbors. He got along famously with people who by type and profession would not get along with one another. He read omnivorously when he had the time, and liked to laugh—even at himself.

No one enjoyed more than he did, for example, the answer given by a young cook from Philadelphia when the Admiral, exhausted by a long, hard inspection tour, was going through the galley of a South Coast base. "How's the chow?" asked the Admiral perfunctorily. "Excellent," said the boy who prepared it, grinning. "Are the men gaining weight?" "Well, sir, I don't exactly know," replied the cook, smiling more broadly. "You see, sir, I don't have to weigh 'em; I just have to feed 'em."

Notwithstanding the palace atmosphere of all Commands, we admired—and liked—Admiral Kirk genuinely. He knew his authority. And could exercise it with flourishes. But in general he managed to take the sting out of the sycophancy which was part of duty. He sincerely cared for his men. He not only won their willing loyalty, but knew how to get the best out of them by using them to their own best advantage.

The London in which we found ourselves with Admiral Kirk during the winter preceding the Invasion was very different from the London of the previous winter. When I had reached it then at the beginning of November in 1942, the war news was still almost wholly bad.

Our landings in Africa were just about to be made. Rommel was at the gates of Alexandria. The Battle of the Atlantic was being fought fiercely against packs of omnivorous U-boats. The losses on the Murmansk run were sometimes as high as 50 per cent. Sicily, Salerno, Anzio, and Italy were a long way off. The Luftwaffe was formidable, undowned, and active. Mussolini was still on his balcony; the Mediterranean a danger zone. The conferences at Casablanca and Teheran had yet to be held. Though fighting magnificently on the defensive, the Russians had not then won their great offensive victories. In the Pacific the tide remained against us. The first Quebec Conference, at which the plans for the European Invasion were discussed one year before it took place, was ten months away.

The hour was black. Fortitude was the fuel most needed by liberty-loving people everywhere. Although the British were stubbornly convinced that the war would some day be over and that the Allies would eventually win it, Fortress Europe still seemed a Brobdingnagian Bastille in a period when the calendar omitted the Fourteenth of July.

The news, in fact, was so bleak during my first two or three bewildered days in London that, late one afternoon, on my way back to my hotel, I vividly remember hearing an old man who was selling newspapers cry, "Buy a paper tonight! Please do! Really good news for a change tonight." This was the day when General Alexander and General Montgomery had begun the long drive which was to push Rommel out of Africa. A lot more good news was to follow.

If events had by-passed us in London during the winter of 1942-43, we all knew we were included in the action last winter. London was the center of gigantic doings. No one who was there could avoid this realization. The fact that something was coming —that something had to come—that the moment was approaching for that mysterious something known as the Invasion, revitalized everyone's living. The Invasion was in every newspaper; on everyone's tongue; uppermost in every mind and heart. Although we knew we had reached what Mr. Churchill had described as "the end of the beginning," we were all eager for the beginning of the end. We were keyed up to it.

In such a London most of us felt transplanted. None more so than the middle-aged. We, in particular, had our moments of

Old England—Young America

feeling as transplanted as the full-grown trees which struggle for life in front of New York's St. Patrick's Cathedral. We were uprooted not because of London, but because we were in London in wartime and in uniform, without our families and our regular lives.

We learned much from the uprooting, even if at times we knew the emotions of having been sent to Culver in our forties. If we blinked at the sunlight of such an experience, it was because as specialists we were mine mules who for years had seen no light except the rays which had happened to penetrate our own particular shafts.

The experience had its high values. If it narrowed our living, it widened our sympathies and standards. For one thing, it bent wills, unindoctrinated and self-indulgent, to discipline. For another, it taught us Reservists in our middle years how to get along with our naval superiors no less than with men twenty years younger than ourselves. Both lessons required learning.

To look at a man's sleeves before looking at his face is to judge men in a way unacknowledged by the psychologists. To be silent when your profession has been words, to have no opinions when opinions have been your bread, or to be serious when you ache to laugh is not easy. But doubtless it is good for the soul no less than for the Service. To have to respect—and obey— a man because of the braid he wears likewise requires readjustment.

So does constant contact with the young. It is at once the most healthy and rejuvenating of experiences—and the most aging. It can make you feel equipped at one moment to get "in the groove," and at the next suddenly lodge you behind the steering wheel of an Electric.

The young take to modern warfare with an aptitude middle-aged novices cannot hope to equal. Having less to forget, they learn the more rapidly. Their responses are instinctive. Their physical stamina is infinitely greater. Their spirits are fresher because life has not yet dismayed them.

Quite naturally, they take for granted inventions, such as the

54

airplane, the radio, or radar, which to the middle-aged, if the truth must out, have a perverse way of remaining somewhat incredible inventions. They assume the airplane, as we assumed the automobile, as our great-grandfathers assumed the horse and buggy. They are machine-minded; natural technocrats. Their fears are few, their hopes many.

To get along with the young, you must chaperon your memories vigilantly. These betray your vintage sooner than anything else. You must bury half of your life most of the time. Otherwise, you are a bore, a relic, or, crueler still, an anachronism. The young have as much difficulty placing the familiar events of twenty years ago as the middle-aged have in identifying the band leaders, the planes, or mechanized equipment of the last few years.

I still recall the vacant looks on the faces of some young lieutenants at whose table I was sitting when I happened to mention Marilyn Miller as confidently as one of them had mentioned Ginger Rogers. Only one man present had ever heard of her. He was my contemporary. And, after this, doubly valued as a friend. In desperation we formed a two-membered Marilyn Miller Club where we could talk without embarrassment or explanation about the dead we had known, the living we had seen, and the books we had read when those around us were still reading *Peter Rabbit*.

Even so, the young are the best of teachers as well as the best of pupils. Those of them who have traveled far in this war have a war-born wisdom and age of their own. They not only know what we have forgotten but what we can never hope to know. As a rule, they so reaffirmed our faith in man that some of us, middle-aged and hence supposedly cynical, began to feel like reformed Rasputins.

We could not avoid, however, the questions raised in our minds by the young men, especially by the young mechanics and the boys from the filling stations, now dressed in blue or khaki, who were manning our ships, emerging from our tanks at maneuvers, or stationed at our Bomber Commands.

55

They, and their kind, were the indispensable men of the moment. They were saving America and the world. They were the real Tommy Atkinses of the threatened hour. No one could deny that this was, first of all, a young man's war and, secondly, a mechanic's war.

These young men with their irreplaceable knowledge and skill revealed, without meaning to, the nature of modern warfare by confessing its necessities. By so doing, they gave those of us who were university-trained in the liberal arts disquieting causes for reflection.

Look over the professions included on a list such as the Selective Service Occupational Questionnaire. Those brought up on the Humanities and hoping, even so, to have some value as citizens will stumble upon a discouraging discovery.

What are a country's needs when tested? Writers, painters, poets, musicians, artists, journalists? Or people rich in knowledge, or valued for their aesthetic perceptions? Or distinguished for their public acts in government? Or college-guided in the cultural blooms of a civilization? These men can play and have played, and have played gladly and well, their part in the war effort. But no mention is made of them. In the judgment of an harassed government, they are irrelevances. Or, at best, luxuries and superfluities.

What America needs to survive—just now—are obviously the nimble fingers and brains of her airplane fabric workers, her pilots, and airplane woodworkers; her angle punchers and shearers; her armorers, asbestos workers, and blacksmiths; her blasters and cable splicers; her crane operators and dredgers; her drill press operators and dynamic balancers; her electricians and engravers; her explosive operators and dairy farmers; her finishers in the rolling mills and her flanging press operators; her galvanizers of steel and iron and her hammersmiths; her lathe operators and her lead burners; her lumber graders and locomotive repairmen; her melters, metallurgists, and millwrights; her printers, riggers, and scarfers; her sheet-metal workers and steam fitters; her thread grinders and tool dressers; her weavers, welders,

The Rhino's Feet

What Makes the Rhino Ferries Run

and wiredrawers.

Even on the Selective Service list of desired "professional" or scientific workers, the liberal arts are omitted. The wartime importance of accountants, naval architects, chemists, dentists, engineers of every kind, geographers, geophysicists, mathematicians, physicians, psychologists, social workers, statisticians, and veterinarians is apparent. And some mild encouragement may perhaps be had from the inclusion on such a list of lawyers and historians.

But such a questionnaire is not comforting to those thinking beyond the immediate war needs of our survival to a peacetime justification of that survival. A nation writes its autobiography in the uses to which it puts its leisure no less than in the products of its industries. Science must serve a higher purpose than saving men merely for factories. Or for war.

In England, as everywhere in the world, the needs of the war at hand loomed just then larger than the worries of a remote peace. In the mud and rain at the bases and in the black-outs in London, many young and middle-aged Americans alike, regardless of whether they were grade-school graduates or college-trained, knew the horrors of homesickness and loneliness. "The British," William McDermott of the *Cleveland Plain Dealer* once observed in Naples, "the British at least know they are fighting *for* a threatened island; most Americans seem to know only that they are fighting *against* homesickness."

When the Russians were advancing with sensational speed last winter, and the British and Americans were more or less standing still in Europe, some of us concocted an overfacile explanation for this. The Russians, we argued, were a magnificent peasant people, at least a hundred and fifty years nearer the American frontier in hardihood and living standards than were we or the British. Since they were unsoftened by our standards, we contended, they naturally fought better than we did. They were so many mechanized Daniel Boones and Simon Kentons, with sawed-off machine guns, bazookas, rockets, and airplanes at their disposal. The notable thing about the British and Americans, we said pompously, was not that they advanced slowly, but that, considering the degree of their civilization, they were able to fight as well as they did.

It was a pretty theory when advanced over discouraged drinks at the Connaught, that Edwardian hotel which to some of us was the pleasantest place for foregathering we found in London. The only trouble with our theory was that it was not true. Ultimately, and in spite of our gadgets and our kindlinesses, our men were to do no less well. They were to move forward so swiftly that one still wonders how they managed to excel the Germans at their own game of Blitzkrieg.

Americans in England lived on letters from home. They were an essential part of their diet. They also lived on boxes sent overseas from time to time by thoughtful families.

The human palate rebels at taking out final papers in a foreign land. The difference between English and American cooking must always have presented the governors of the English-speaking Union with one of their gravest problems. Full-grown men, who had abandoned all hopes of ever seeing an egg again, developed in England the kind of craving for samples of American fruits, cheeses, candies, and canned goods which is usually associated with expectant mothers.

The boxes sent from home, like the weekly supply of candies and cookies bought at the Post Exchange, brought out an alarming bootlegger secretiveness in the most straightforward of Americans. That was, if they were generous enough to share their loot.

"Come in," a well-fed, gray-haired officer would whisper, furtively closing the door to his flat. With a shushing finger placed against his lips, he would thereupon announce, "I have a box from home. And . . . ," he would add, looking around as if for Federal agents, "some Fig Newtons."

A few seconds later, drooling men, who thought they had eaten their last Fig Newtons twenty-five years before, would fall upon a box of them like a pack of wolves, emitting all the appropriate exclamations which are the property of connoisseurs, and in general relishing the stolen pleasures of an "after-lights spread" at school. No pressed duck at the Tour d'Argent ever tasted better

59

than did these Fig Newtons, or the food in the boxes from home.

A change in diet was just one of the readjustments which Americans had to make in England. Certainly no two people are at once as similar and dissimilar as are the English and the Americans. Mr. Shaw once insisted that we were two peoples separated by the same language. Perhaps, if our tongues were as similar in their accents as are our hearts, our understanding of one another would be greater. The tragedy is that in our eagerness to relish the differences which divide us, we both overlook the similarities which unite us, though for the sake of the world's happiness these alone are what matter.

All of us approached England with an England already in our minds. It was either an England we had known and thought we knew, or an England we had heard, though never thought, about. It was an England which her literature and our travel had made real, or which our funny papers and stage types had made ridiculous. In either case it was a mythical kingdom, bearing no relation to the changed England of the war years.

If you talked to many of our men, including those who frankly admitted they had known little about England, or to our officers, including those who were guilty of the fatal tourist's mistake of thinking they knew a lot, you realized how odd were the preconceptions we Americans brought with us. These could not have been odder unless they had been the notions entertained by equivalent Englishmen on the subject of America and Americans.

The untraveled go on the most dangerous journeys, because they are never confronted with what would change their minds. The only travelers as dangerous as those who form their opinions without leaving home are those who might just as well have stayed there, because their preconceptions and their prejudices (for or against) are the heaviest luggage they carry.

Among our men were those, of course, whose elderly aunts had, so to speak, been snubbed by an English lady on a street car in Portland or Kansas City. And those whose uncles had been smiled upon by King George and Queen Mary at a large garden party given at Buckingham Palace some twenty years ago. These men had been conditioned accordingly. They arrived mobilized for snubs or smiles and were not only avid in their search for them, but disappointed if they did not receive them.

The England some of our men brought with them to England seemed to be an odd jumble of many things. It was a potpourri of grandfather's tales (as if England had not altered since grandfather had gone there for two weeks in 1907); of fox-hunting prints; of Pickwickian expectations; of vaudeville sketches and musical comedy lampoons about English lords sporting monocles and walrus mustaches; of father's recollections of the last war, when his outfit had been stationed next to a British unit or when he had seen *Chu Chin Chow* during a London leave; of Henry VIII as Charles Laughton and Queen Victoria as Helen Hayes or Anna Neagle; of *Ivanhoe,* Kipling, and *Little Lord Fauntleroy;* of William Shakespeare at the World's Fair in Chicago or in a Nebraska classroom, or of Robert Taylor at Oxford.

Strangely intermingled with such travel documentation were hazy and contradictory memories which ranged from Braddock's defeat, the Boston Tea Party, the Declaration of Independence, and the burning of Washington right down to newsreels of the Blitz, Dunkerque, the King, and Mr. Churchill; to Ed Murrow's London broadcasts; to such movies as *In Which We Serve, Mrs. Miniver,* and *Good-bye, Mr. Chips;* to such a poem as *White Cliffs;* or to such a song as "There'll Always Be an England."

Our first search, like theirs, was, naturally enough, for oddity. We wanted England to be English (whatever that meant), though we judged it for not being American. They wanted us to be Americans (whatever that meant), though they judged us for not being like themselves. We hoped they would be quaint, top-lofty, reserved, and either ducal or old-retainerish; they hoped we would be breezy, boastful, boisterous, and just a touch red-skinned.

Both expectations were surprisingly antiquated. Many of the English would have been the happier in their hearts had we been a cross between *Brewster's Millions,* William S. Hart, and Al

Capone. Many of our men were secretly disappointed because the English were not more like Dickens, *Ruggles of Red Gap,* and our comics.

Some of our servicemen approached the British with minds torn between a wholehearted admiration for Britain's war record and an unconscious recollection of what their grandfathers had laughed at in Mark Twain. Many Britishers saw us, without meaning to do so, through the eyes of Mrs. Trollope, even though they hoped to identify us with our music or our movies. If, at the outset, both of us wanted to laugh good-naturedly at the other, it was because ridicule is everyone's first line of defense against the strange.

We, in the Services, who were there in wartime could never pretend to know England well. We were too chained to our Commands to enjoy even a tourist's freedom. The British were too grimly occupied with the war to form opinions which were more than individually accurate about us. When we met our kind among them, they were our kind; and passports only kept the conversation going. If we made friends, they forgot we were Americans as rapidly as we forgot they were British. We ceased to be nationals, except for the fun of argument, and became people.

Still, we could no more escape the larger, indefinable differences than the English could. Generalizations about nations have a stubborn way of retaining their elements of truth, however false or misleading they may be. It amused, and sometimes relieved, us to indulge in these generalizations, even as it must have often amused, and relieved, the English to do the same thing. Doubtless, in the British fashion, we found much pleasure in noting the superficial differences. There were new and unsuspected traits to be observed, however, no less than the expected characteristics.

Though well-intentioned and in most ways helpful, the brochures we were all handed, and the lectures to which we listened in the sardine comfort of our transports when nearing England, erred in being too thorough. Their catalogue of national differences made us self-conscious and tended to persuade those who were visiting the UK for the first time that they were Gullivers about to set foot on an incredible land.

Some Americans never got beyond the easy stage of observing that the English must be a strange people because they do not speak as we do; because they drive on the left-hand side of the road; because everyone of whom a direction is asked while driving or walking invariably says, after indicating it, "You carn't possibly miss it," which is precisely what you can and do proceed to do; because their trains are unlike ours; because their money is different; and because, though they make better tea than we do, their coffee, to put it mildly, is nothing to write home about except in sorrow.

Other Americans, whose chief contact with the British was with their telephone operators, did not become Anglophiles. To put through a call in wartime London was more than a chore; it was a profession. The operators had a way of treating the telephone as if it were not here to stay—which was just the opposite of their attitude toward you.

The fact that in England an apartment was called a flat, a bartender a barman, a bouncer a chucker-out, a conductor a guard, a cop a bobby, an elevator a lift, a lawyer a solicitor, a saloon a pub, the subway the underground, or a truck a lorry created only the most negligible static in the interchange of ideas. But there were differences which caught the ear, the eye, and the mind.

Although our average sailors and soldiers appeared to be larger, stronger, more self-possessed, and better educated than their Cockney cousins, the same thing was not true of our Junior Officers. We could not help noticing that the average cultivated Britisher, at any age, seemed about a century older than the equivalent American. Not in looks, because the English can remain Romney cherubs in the pinkness of their skins and the clearness of their eyes until they reach for their last whisky and soda. No. But a hundred years older in worldliness. From babyhood they had inhaled the atmosphere of the Old World, and we the atmosphere of the New. This had aged their spirits even as it had

63

caused us to resist maturity.

Somehow, they seemed more basted in world affairs than we were. Their minds had never halted at their island coasts, which were their natural frontiers. The world has been needed to hold their nationals and their nation. Both their thinking and their phrasing made this clear. They, too, may have had no more than country-club minds, but their country clubs, under whatever names they traveled, had the specious allure of faraway places.

If the British had lost the spiritual freshness which was ours, it was because the global dilemmas, which we as a people were just then beginning to face in earnest, had for centuries been commonplaces to their forebears. They were born believing not that the world was their oyster, but that its pearls were their inheritance. This explained their difficulties and some of our difficulties with them.

As a rule, they hid their enthusiasms as zealously as we exposed ours. Where they seemed to us blasé because incredulous, we must have seemed to them naïve because of our anxiety to believe everything that both we and they said. The more knowing among them may have been denied the joys of wonder, but they were spared the pains of disenchantment.

It was not that they were disillusioned. It was merely that they appeared to have been born without illusions. Obviously, they had long been settlers in regions of thought and enterprise which we were still approaching as discoverers. They were surprised mainly by our surprise. They faced facts as naturally as we embraced ideals. We were the more material people, they the more practical. Although they did not have our genius for mechanization, our absorption in gadgets, or our desire for small comforts, they got along well enough without them. Figures mattered as much to them as things did to us. Their practicality extended to their ideals.

The Empire was more with them than our government had been with us. They had a gift for remembering the Empire's future business while not forgetting their own momentary pleasures. Although their young naval officers had encircled the globe, they had never traveled only as tourists. They had visited the hot spots, the post-card places, and the museums with our avidity. But they had also made mental notes of harbors, fortifications, and local industries. Just in case.

Most of them were people whose lives were made secure by professions and enriched by avocations, whereas the majority of us, even if we had professions, liked to pretend they were no more than jobs. They had no false modesty, but we had less candid pride.

They were not embarrassed, in our fashion, by knowledge and did not share our inexplicable fear that strangers might suspect us of having had a university education. The cricket fans among them, who were officers, were as fond of quoting poetry as our officers, who were baseball addicts, were pleased by remembering scores. When they quoted English poetry, they knew it, old and new and by the page, and did not halt, as we did, with the first lines of *Snow-Bound* or *The Midnight Ride of Paul Revere*.

Though we appeared to have the more fertile minds, they enjoyed the greater felicity of phrase and the greater conversational stamina. Their education endowed the English with this advantage. They were equipped to sustain the illusion of culture, sometimes where no real culture or insight existed. We were prepared to deny it. Theirs was the smoother patter. They could be as suave in advancing their bromides as we could be gauche in establishing our originalities.

They could talk well—publicly no less than privately—even when they had nothing to say; whereas we, so easy in our small talk, usually stammered when we had the bigger things on our minds. Their only trouble as conversationalists was that sometimes they were more fond of telling than of asking. Their lack of curiosity was not a sign that they had no desire to know. It was a betrayal that they thought they knew already. This was one of their signs of national age.

They were the best of epitaph writers, even if they failed signally where they ought to have excelled—namely, in the snobbish overwriting which spoils the noblest lines on the Tomb of the

65

Unknown Soldier. But they had not been brought up on the King James Bible for nothing. Their statesmen have always shown a greater talent than have ours for paraphrasing the Testaments when they have wished to spiritualize pragmatic public acts.

The English were planners where we were improvisers. They thought in terms of fifty years where we thought in terms of a normal presidential term, if indeed we thought that far. They lacked our gusto as surely as we lacked their equability. We were volatile where they were traditional, and unpredictable where they were certain.

If we amused them by always rushing off somewhere, even if we had nothing to do when we got there, they could infuriate us by remaining calm and unmoved, in spite of the fact that they ought to have got going long ago. Although their minds appeared to move more slowly than ours, this was not necessarily because they were slower in their thinking. It may have been because they were thinking ahead. Their leisure was as much a proof of their self-control as our energy was of our spontaneity.

They respected their right to stand in a queue as much as we rejoiced in ours to shove, or be shoved, into a bus. This was just one of the ways in which they confessed their greater love for law and order.

They were class-conscious, not because they wanted to do away with class distinctions, but because they liked the settled feeling it gave them to know that those who had got ahead would stay there. In laughter they were apt to be as estranged from us as *The New Yorker* is from *Punch*. Their fondness for the drawings in the latter revealed how close they were to the illustrator of *Peter Ibbetson* and *Trilby* in the visual techniques even of their humor.

They were men living in a world run for men, whereas we were men temporarily removed from a world run for women. This may have explained the different degrees in our male assurance.

The old, and insufferable, arrogance of the British had largely gone. It had disappeared with the pre-Singapore Englishman, for whose mentality Britain had little respect since it had cost them

66

so much. I looked in vain for the kind of Englishwoman, equipped with the nudging elbows out of which Empire is made, whom I remembered with alarm from the thirties. She had passed through a line of Americans waiting to disembark at a Swedish port, saying, "If you'll just let me go first, I'll be out of your way." The unamazing thing was that she had not been stopped. No one had had the temerity to question logic seemingly so safe from doubt.

The British had been through hell. They had come out of it with a disarming humility. Instead of assuming that they would be admired merely because they were British, they had developed a sincere desire to be liked as people. They could not have been more hospitable, although they had little for themselves, or more generous when they were experiencing harder times than America has ever dreamed of knowing. They showed the warm hearts of hosts who wanted their guests made comfortable in spite of every sacrifice. They had the patience of Job and the realism of a people who recognized that the world's liking was now one of their needs. It was only with one another that they remained snobs. They would have thought the less of themselves had they not done so.

Regardless of their love of titles and traditions, no visitor could fail to realize that the British love of freedom was fierce and undying. One perceived, however slowly, that England had not only been through hell; she had undergone another and much further reaching Bloodless Revolution. Instead of making her reactionary, the worst of wars had produced the Beveridge Report and the bill for educational reform. Much as she prized her Court Circular, and Tory as she was thought to be, she was much nearer to a socialized state than we were.

Her people of all classes had taken their sacrifices and their labors for granted. German bombers had seen to this. England's workers had made England's cause theirs. Her aristocrats, though curtailed in their estates, were not worried about their future. They had possessions within themselves which they could not lose and which the country valued. Once again they had met

67

wholeheartedly their responsibilities as the governing.

The intermingling of the British and American Armed Forces was friendly. There were fights, of course. They were due to our higher pay, to sex, to drink, to shared tactlessness, to old prejudices, and to the boredom—common in the Services—which makes any brawl welcome until the real fight comes along.

The pity was that fraternization was not more common between the enlisted men of both countries. In general, they were content to travel with their own nationals, though many of them were authoritative on the subject of English girls. Our officers were more experimental. Their friendships with the British were easy, profitable, and delightful. One's hope was that in victory England would not lose the new virtues acquired in her dark hours.

It was impossible to be in any part of Great Britain in wartime without respecting her people for their courage. "England has always possessed the armament that she needed. She has always fought with the weapons required for success. She fought with mercenaries as long as mercenaries sufficed. But she also dipped into the most valuable blood of her entire nation whenever such a sacrifice alone was able to bring about victory. But the determination to fight and the tenacity and unflinching conduct always remained the same." These observations were Hitler's. Neither he nor we can disagree with them today.

The differences between the English and Americans were easy to find. So were the similarities. They ran deeper; they underlay all the diverting superficial cleavages. We did not have to look very far for them in England. That they were compelling and ineffable was best illustrated by our presence there. And by the joint indignations which had once again brought us side by side.

Chapter V

Children of Daedalus

As I climbed into the plane, I found myself staring at the German pilot. He was a skinny, pimply faced boy of seventeen; blond enough to please the *Führer,* and as frightened and curious as any prisoner of his age would naturally be. With another German, a private, noticeable only because of his uniform, and with two amused Italians, he was being flown from Casablanca to London, guarded by a trim British officer.

At an airport in Africa; the whole way north; when we landed in Scotland; and, most particularly, as we flew low over England, heading south for London, I could not take my eyes or thoughts off this German boy, the pilot.

At Casa when he and his fellows, segregated behind a counter and covered by the tommy gun of a nonchalant GI, had stood in a corner, four against so many, I had watched him with mixed emotions. He was not prepossessing. Far from it. He was of high-school age and zoot-suit mentality; an adolescent whose dangling jaw advertised adenoids and whose splotched skin had barely been introduced to a razor.

Instead of being arrogant or evil, he was a very ordinary kid who, in happier times, might have been indispensable as a farm-hand in Bavaria. All things considered, including his age and whereabouts, he was putting on a good show of self-possession. His nervousness expressed itself chiefly in the minnow-like dart-ings of his blue eyes and by the frequency with which he mois-tened his lips or drove the knuckles of his right hand deep into the palm of his left.

69

To watch him scan a poster showing the uniforms and insignia of the enemy, and then to check on that poster's accuracy merely by looking at him, was odd enough. To turn in the midst of a conversation with the American or Britisher next to you, and see him standing before another poster, reading DON'T TALK—THE ENEMY IS LISTENING, was odder still.

In the night hours on the flight north across the Bay of Biscay, I wondered if he would share our feelings should a German plane attack our unarmed transport. Would the mere act of being fired on make our enemy his? Or would he, in the best tradition of the scenario writers, welcome such an attack, regardless of his own safety?

As we neared Scotland, he pressed his shiny nose against the window with the eagerness of any youthful tourist. When we had changed planes and were heading south, he could scarcely remain in his seat. He would jump up from time to time to get a better view. He began to scrutinize the terrain. His interest in it was as professional as the interest he had shown when he had checked our pilot's landings and our take-off.

England fascinated him as Germany would have fascinated us. And why not? Though seemingly amused by the thatched roofs, the Norman towers, the large estates, and the cloisonné of the fields as they slid under us, he was trained to observe other features of the English landscape.

He missed none of the airfields which dot the countryside. With narrowed, appraising eyes he looked at every British or American plane that came near us. He cocked his head to notice all the indications of antiaircraft guns he could find. He noted it whenever we passed over concentrations of our troops. Or convoys on the roads below. Or any signs of ammunition dumps.

Regardless of what might be in store for him, this was plainly a charabanc ride aloft. He was not seeing England in the night. When he looked back, no trail of flames marked his course. He did not have to elude fighters or take cover in a cloud. No flak came up to greet him. No rockets were on hand to welcome him. The sun, not the moon, was his beacon. This was a new kind of

70

busman's holiday. As we neared London, he pressed his forehead against the pane to discover proofs of bomb damage. Whenever he found them, he elbowed the German private beside him, nodding his head in approval.

When at the airfield he was led away with his companions, I thought I had seen the last of this German boy of seventeen. But in February and March, during fiercer nights of the Baby Blitz, I was to see him again. Many times. I could not put him out of my mind.

His reappearances were made long before the first robot bombs had fallen on London; those bombs which, by showering southern England, should have made clear to us at home in far-off America that, if or when there is another war, the physical immunity which our cities have enjoyed in this one is a blessing they will have enjoyed for the last time. The robot planes I never saw. I was to miss their coming by one day. But during the period of the waiting all of us in England were to get to know enemy planes only too well.

Before I had seen this young German, enemy planes to me—quite foolishly—had always been machines. Mere machines. Mighty machines. Nighthawks of chromium. As impersonal as shells in the air. Even our planes, once aloft, had always swallowed up for me the airmen I knew personally and had seen step into them.

When, on nights beyond number during my two winters in London, I had heard German planes skim the chimney pots or drone their way with pulsing motors far above the city, I had always thought of them as divorced from men. Even when they had flown low over us off Sicily, annihilating the darkness with their flares and dropping their bombs on the water near by, or when I had seen them shot down by day near Scoglitti, I had continued to think of them as planes; frightful, beautiful, powerful, relentless; the air arm of the enemy, not an enemy; the mailed fist, not the human fingers inside of it.

This pimply faced adolescent was to destroy for me the Frankenstein notion. Although he was to subtract from my awe of the

71

machine, he was not to lessen my dread of it. In my eyes, he only increased its horror.

In the future whenever an "Alert" obliterated sleep, and ack-ack stitched the sky, or the near-by rocket guns syringed the ears with horror, I was to see this boy at the controls. Seeing him, I became the more perplexed; the more indignant.

It perplexed me to have him dare to function as destiny's stand-in. It infuriated me to know that if a pair of hands, as young and clumsy as his, just happened to release a bomb over the building in which I lived, his gesture would be my life. It angered me to realize that should he, without thinking, feed his engine a drop or two of gas, he would spare us in our building but reach out for life in another. It outraged me to realize that this youth had under his dominion the age and associations of Westminster Abbey. That the architectural glories of the Banqueting Hall were as nothing compared to his whim. And that every monument and home over which he flew lay, because of his passing, in the shadow of death. We were all at his mercy; the living and the dead; the past and the present; the future, too.

There had been a time during the initial months of our first war winter in London when some of us, from a purely selfish point of view, had looked forward to an air raid. This was when we had felt by-passed by events. It was when we needed some such challenge to restore our waning self-respect.

During November, December, and the first half of January in '42 and '43, we had lived among the proofs of London's sufferings. But in these sufferings we had not shared. Although the illustrations were all around us, we had not experienced the text. We, in uniform, wanted to be able to face as equals the British civilians who, without their choosing, had been engulfed by the hazards and horrors which, by our choice, should have been ours.

Then, at last, an air raid had come. Each man's first air raid, like each man's first baby, is a special, though not a blessed, event. This one had come on January 17, to be exact, on a Sunday evening when Richard Watts, Jr., that veteran of the sirens in Chungking and Madrid, happened to have flown over from the

OWI in Dublin for a visit.

The two of us, as old friends, and erstwhile dramatic critics, were happy to find ourselves once again together for another show. If he enjoyed the role of mentor, and played it well, I liked the part of pupil, and thank him even now for having introduced me to that odd, but genuine, form of sociability which air raids can induce, so long as the hits are not too close.

We were having drinks before dinner in a friend's apartment at the Dorchester Hotel. The Dorchester, with its rich refugees and general atmosphere of unthreatened luxury, is, let me quickly add, the least Nelsonian of surroundings from which to send a message to Emma. It is the last place anyone brought up on *The Red Book of Heroes* would choose for a take-off into the ultimate.

"There go our planes," our host had observed. Above the talk we could hear their roar. We switched off the lights and parted the black-out curtains to see them. But planes don't sit for their portraits. They had already gone.

"Too bad for Berlin," said someone with a wartime sense of humor. And we all laughed as happily at this as people on either side in a war do laugh when they learn the enemy is in for disaster. The first principle of war is that you do unto others as you would not have them do unto you. The Nazis had inaugurated this particular kind of doing. It was their time to take it now, and the world's good fortune that our Air Forces were at last in a position to pay back. No one could feel sorry for those who had shown no pity for others. Accordingly, we had been happy. And had laughed. In wartime, one laughs at strange things. One has to. There is no other choice.

Our laughs had scarcely died, when the sirens outbayed the hounds of the Baskerville.

"A raid," said someone else, brightly, but without laughing.

Then, with incredible swiftness, the ack-ack opened up. At first it was far away; startling but remote, like the headlines of local interest in the newspapers of a city not your own.

Thereafter, at a plane's speed, the sounds had swept closer and closer, deepening as they approached, leaving more and more echoes in the midriff. Soon the near-by guns were adding to the uproar. For forty-five minutes, the boomings, now distant, now neighborly, swept back and forth across the city.

According to connoisseurs, the barrage was the biggest London had so far put up. Those caught on the streets said the flak had fallen like hail.

When the noise was tapering off, we had another drink. Someone played "Heil Right in the Führer's Face" on the Victrola as the crowning joke. And we all went down to dinner, feeling that peculiar exhilaration for which the nearness of danger can be responsible, and which, for all I know, may be only a reverse manifestation of fear.

At five the next morning, long after Dick Watts had returned as an inveterate newspaperman to the Savoy, there had been another raid. Since my bed at the Athenaeum Court was under a long window, I got up. Glass and bombs do not mix. Even I knew that. After having first looked at the slip of sky visible above my courtyard air shaft, and having seen that it was alive with flares, tracers, and the crossed beams of searchlights, I had withdrawn to the little hall off my bedroom.

Outside in the main hall was a group of Britishers. They were complaining good-naturedly about the loss of sleep—"beastly bore, dontcha know . . ." And joking about the pajama party Hitler was giving them. They were as audible as only the British can be when they are talking to one another. Whatever secrets the English may have, they do not keep in elevators or in restaurants, those two confessionals in which self-consciousness so quickly muffles us in spite of our supposed noisiness as a people. When we talk loud, it is because we want an audience; when the British talk loud, it is because they are unaware they have one.

Forty German planes were said to have come over on this morning raid, compared with the thirty-five which had crossed and recrossed London the evening before. Some of these in the morning attack had flown so low that it was impossible not to hear the uneven whir of their motors.

A year after this, and notwithstanding long intervals of quiet, German planes were still coming over. By this time they had lost their novelty. Not that this made them any more welcome. The more we had seen of them, the less they had appealed to us.

But by then each of us had begun to work out his own individual routine of welcome. This routine was determined by the depth of our slumbers or the altitude of our rooms. The sound sleepers invariably pretended to have slept the sounder on the nights when there were raids. "Oh, was there a raid last night? Didn't hear it," they would say. But some of us insomniacs, whose rooms were perched at the tops of buildings so as to lower our rents, never failed to hear the "Alert" or to be grateful for the "All Clear."

I was then living at 42 Upper Brook Street in an attic room which had never made up its mind whether it was designed for Chatterton or Sara Crewe. As the Germans were fond of dropping incendiaries, and as these had a way of invading one's privacy, and even of becoming bedfellows, without waiting for an invitation, I used to drape my clothes each night on a chair beside my bed. Going to bed knowing there is apt to be a raid at some unpredictable hour is not alarming. It is merely a bore. It is a bore that grows the more boring as time goes on, and when there is a run of raids for several consecutive nights.

Each night or early morning when the siren sounded, I would dress, realizing the "Alert" usually meant a ten-minute breather. At my window I would watch the searchlights trying to find their way through the clouds. And wait to see what the guns would do, assuming the nearness of the firing to be an accurate indication of the nearness of the targets. If the guns near by did not wake up, I would go back to bed.

If they did, I would gather up my most valued possessions and go down to the floor below to awaken a friend who lived there. We would talk and nip with the greatest false merriment until the noises began to come too close. Then we would drop down to the second or fourth floors, where other friends lived. The party would then continue, with everyone laughing uproariously at someone's faintly heard jokes. And with everyone being very—oh, very, very—brave and chin up, though each of us was secretly listening only to the sounds outside and pretending they were the last things on our minds.

What proved that these parties were not quite as successful as they would have been had they been held at more convivial hours and without the orchestration of a raid was that, at the first sounds of the "All Clear," all of us would return to our rooms as promptly as if the clock had just struck midnight on a dormitory of Cinderellas. Or we would stumble out on the roof to see what had happened.

Sometimes the black sky line would be ringed with huge strawberries of fire. Once such a conflagration was only a few blocks away. We went to that fire. Unexploded incendiaries were still sticking in the asphalt of the streets. A stiff wind was blowing the volcanic flames from a corner building to a row of houses across the street. The fire was gradually spreading to the roofs of these houses.

On the bad nights, when there were many fires, London's fire fighters had to establish immediate priorities in salvation, on the basis of the general danger or wartime importance of the buildings threatened or blazing. This night there was a crowd in the street. A fire chief drove up in a car and quickly appraised the situation. Then he drove on to another fire a few blocks away, a fire more menacing to the war effort. The look of resolution on the faces of those Britishers in this crowd as they accepted this decision and watched London burning was something Hitler should have seen.

Although I was in good company during most of the raids, I never developed any fondness for the raids themselves. Nor could I acquire that blasé attitude which dismissed all raids made by five or ten planes as being "mild," insisting that to be newsworthy at least one hundred planes must come over. I never knew of a bomb that fell mildly. I could not forget that a hit usually meant a home. Or that one enemy plane is more than enough if

Alexander P. Russo

London Night Scene

you just happen to be in the wrong place.

I could not abide the notion of a city being indiscriminately attacked. I hated being trapped in a building. I much preferred my air raids on the open bridge of a ship in action. After February I could not rid myself of the image of that adolescent German pilot. He, and the power which he accepted unthinkingly, troubled me the more.

Over England the air lived its own life and brought its own death. It paved its indispensable way for the Invasion. Almost daily we looked up to see our Flying Fortresses and Fighters going out and coming back. Almost nightly we could hear the drone of the RAF heading for the Continent or returning from it. These motors became part of the rhythm of our lives. We began to take them as much for granted as we did the intermittent German raids.

Meanwhile, London continued on her way, ignoring the sky as best she could, but not forgetting the war. Her streets, her hotels and restaurants, her stations and her stores, her factories and her libraries, her schools and her churches and her theatres were all crowded. So were her air raid shelters.

Although almost anything succeeded, the London theatre did not shine. Tired before the war, it was naturally more tired by then. People in no way express their wartime despair more openly than in the little that it takes to amuse them.

The best plays were apt to be revivals or American scripts. Such stand-bys as *Arsenic and Old Lace, My Sister Eileen,* or *Uncle Harry* were on hand in English productions to divert the British and to make Americans feel that Broadway had moved over to Shaftesbury Avenue to greet them. John Gielgud was lending his fine powers to a brilliant revival of *Love for Love*. Contemporary English playwriting was most happily represented by such a farce as Terence Rattigan's *The Sun Shines On*. But, quite properly, the toasts of the town were to the Lunts in *There Shall Be No Night*. To keep up with the rat race of current history, Mr. Sherwood's play by then had Athens rather than Finland as its scene, but in its Greek translation it had gained.

78

London remained undeterred by her wounds. She was at once a city and a city at war. Her newspapers and magazines, though newsprint was cruelly rationed, remained true to the standards that had formerly been theirs. The programs of BBC remained the programs of BBC. The secondhand bookstores were never so crowded, or new books in greater demand. The orators at Hyde Park corner still ventilated their grievances out of doors, often before amused crowds of curious American sailors and soldiers. The women, whose offices had always been the sidewalks of Piccadilly, found their business enjoying a war boom. Regardless of what they may have been called in the past, they were then known by what was probably the more dignified name of "Piccadilly Commandos." The black-outs were the best friends their beauty knew.

Through the rubble in the central hallway in the buildings over which Big Ben towers, the mace continued to head the procession into the Commons. It was followed there by a bewigged and black-gowned elder and a page boy who carried his train. The two of them could have stepped out of *Iolanthe*. If the Commons was then meeting in the House of Lords, and the Lords in a committeeroom, it was because only the walls of the old Commons were now standing. But the procession went on. So did the freedom of debate.

In the months preceding the Invasion, London—and England —refused to regard the raids of the Luftwaffe as more than impudent and tiresome interruptions. I kept wondering if the German pilot I had seen on the flight north from Casa had come to realize this, now that he was a prisoner in England.

Once I had spent a week-end with Lieutenant Commander Berger at an American Bomber Command. Our hosts were two charming young Americans. They had given us an excellent Saturday night of good talk and drink. They, and those around them, had faces which refused to choose an age. They were seventeen when they laughed, and forty when they gave or received a command.

Our hosts did not happen to go on the next day's mission. They made it possible for us to sit in on the briefing and watch the take-off in the early morning mist. We waited for the return and saw the field fill with boys, all of whose faces were turned skyward, when the squadron was due. We watched the vacancies in the returning formations. At the interrogation we looked away from the long tables, which, though set, were empty and at which no Intelligence Officers were now needed. We heard a red-headed kid, fresh from his plane, confess his youth by saying with his lips trembling, when he heard a friend had been shot down, "Oh, no. Jim can't be dead. You see, we roomed together at school." As if that were enough to halt death. Later in the week the thank-you notes I had written to our young hosts were returned to me, marked "Missing."

In the spring, not long before the Invasion, I was at the bar in the Dorchester with Ernie Pyle. Two American pilots recognized him at once, and were properly excited at seeing him, because no man in the Armed Forces is more deeply loved than he is.

"It's a funny war," said one of the young pilots to Ernie Pyle. "Here I am this afternoon in London, having a drink in a super-civilized place like this and going to the theatre tonight. And this morning I was out on a short mission across the Channel, dropping bombs to beat hell and killing everyone in sight. I can't figure it out."

Chapter VI

Back to Methuselah

It was in the nature of a pilgrimage. The April sky was cloudless over Hertfordshire, and the English countryside all greens and blossoms and smiling proofs of life which mocked the approaching days of death.

Ayot St. Lawrence was our destination.

Does the name mean nothing to you? Does it ring no bells; no liberty bells such as Ferney would have rung anywhere for troubled people in the eighteenth century indebted to the dauntless independence of Voltaire's mind? Then you are no Shavian and have not guessed the excitement and the curiosity in our hearts.

Surely as a reader you must have stumbled upon Ayot St. Lawrence. Although it is only an hour from London, reaching it in print can take a longer time. In the theatre you by-pass it. But in the library (certainly you remember it now), it has written "Finis" to the Grand Tour through many a Shavian preface.

Even nowadays readers—or rereaders—are apt to come upon it breathless. Even nowadays they are apt to reach it with their prejudices more jostled than the veiled hats of early motorists. They arrive blinking from the relentless sanity of a mind admitting no hour except noon. After the jolts to which they have been subjected on the way, they tend to feel as if they had been reading the Book of Revelation on a roller coaster.

Behind us now were the terrifying night noises of the Baby Blitz, the bleak ink-filled hours of the black-outs, and a bruised London. The sunshine and fresh air we greeted as no more than proper symbols. Because on a free afternoon (another symbol), the three of us—Lieutenant Bundy [1] and an Irrepressible Virginian and I—were heading for a place which we could never imagine as having known a black-out, inasmuch as Mr. Shaw was its First Citizen.

In wartime it is not only threatened cities which seek the security of a black-out. The human mind, in its play of reason, at least most reasons save the major one, goes into eclipse. It has to It has no other choice. The need for military objectives eliminates the luxury of objectivity. When the hurricane is howling through your house, any treatise on air currents is bound to seem an irrelevance, if not an impertinence. The passions of war number dispassion among the enemy.

Certain questions, simple enough in peacetime, cannot be asked even of oneself, and, if asked, expect no answers. The color scale of thought dwindles into black and white. Indeed, the only easy feature of this long, difficult, and bloody struggle is that for most of us never has white been whiter or black blacker.

But what about Mr. Shaw? What about the Elderly Gentleman who has always seen red when the world sees black and to whom nothing is either white or black? Would the supporting orthodoxies of our thinking be safe with him? To his high credit no orthodoxies ever have been. What could one of the globe's few professional Wise Men say about a world forced hourly to demonstrate its lack of wisdom by destruction?

As intermixed meadows and suburbs slipped by, and the talk skimmed hummingbird-wise over many subjects, I could not help thinking back to the wars Mr. Shaw's mind has survived, and the warfare furiously waged by, and against, him during the last war.

God knows, thought I, his old eyes have looked out often enough upon a world which has expressed its sickness in battle. When he spoke at the Metropolitan Opera House in 1933, he confessed that our Civil War was his first memory. He was four when it began, and eight when he heard of Lincoln's assassination. He and wars have never got along. They could scarcely be expected to do so.

[1] Lieutenant, now Captain, MacGeorge Bundy, USA, Admiral Kirk's military aide.

Devon Our Target

He was already red-bearded and well known when the Boer War taxed British arms and patience. He was celebrated when he scandalized "right thinkers" by suggesting in *Arms and the Man* that chocolate is more necessary to the soldier than the gun he carries. He was world-famous and gray when during the last conflict he infuriated the English by dashing off his *Common Sense about the War*.

To most men, including those incapable of it, pure reason is a peacetime privilege, eyed with suspicion even then. In wartime the moths fly away in horror from its flame. Who knows but that by so doing they prove themselves wiser than the wisest Wise Men? When desperate mortals, prepared to die for an idea, however hazily understood, demand for that idea's safety that no neutrals exist among their neighbors, the impartial truth is more than most can tolerate, especially when it is as paradoxically and humorously stated as if no tragic crisis existed.

The man who persists in thinking his own thoughts runs the sniper's risks when conventional patriots have surrendered theirs. "The Nag Sedition was your mother, and Perversity begot you; Mischief was your midwife and Misrule your nurse, and Unreason brought you up at her feet—no other ancestry and rearing had you—(you) freakish homunculus germinated outside of lawful procreation." Thus Mr. Shaw's old friend, Henry Arthur Jones, had fulminated against him during the last war. In his anger and his outrage Mr. Jones was not alone.

H. G. Wells had dubbed Shaw's behavior that of "an idiot child laughing in a hospital." Mr. Shaw's fellow playwrights had demanded his resignation from the Dramatists' Club. W. J. Locke had refused to stay in the same room with him. Even actors had declined to be photographed with him. Once-doting readers clamored for his beard if not his blood.

What had Mr. Shaw said? Very little for which he was not forgiven when peace found him resaying it in *Heartbreak House*. Very little for which he was not praised when the years of disillusionment had settled upon the world. The daring independence of *What I Really Wrote about the War* was as applauded in

84

1932 as it was condemned and despised during the war years.

In peacetime the iconoclasts and the court jesters come back into their own. In wartime they are fated to exist at their own and everyone else's peril. What the conventional have always found doubly hard to forgive in Mr. Shaw is his habit of saying serious things gaily. They read him, unable to determine whether he is a philosopher or a buffoon, and are appalled by the suspicion that he may be both.

During a war, soldiers, sailors, and marines are both expected and demanded to show physical courage. But in wartime, when salvation lies in the mass movements of massed men, the moral courage of a mind insisting upon its singularity naturally goes unappreciated. Mr. Shaw's intellect has always remained as undrafted as his body. The only certainty about him has always been that he will be different; the only predictable feature that he will be unpredictable.

"You may demand moral courage from me to any extent," he had once said, "but when you start shooting and knocking one another about, I claim the coward's privilege and take refuge under the bed. My life is too valuable to be machine-gunned." Although this may be a statement Falstaffian in its realism, and betraying more courage than most medal-wearers could muster, it could hardly be expected to be understood by the expendables who, by being machine-gunned, make it safe for the contrary-minded to think their contrary thoughts. Mr. Shaw had realized his courage. Being Mr. Shaw he had of course appreciated it. "I have been giving exhibitions of moral courage far surpassing anything achieved in the field," said he, "but so far I have not received the V.C.; in fact sarcastic suggestions that I should receive the iron one have not been lacking."

I could not help thinking of these Shavian skirmishes, well-known to all readers of Shaw or Hesketh Pearson, as in the midst of an even more awful and ruthless war we sped toward Ayot St. Lawrence.

Almost before I knew it, it came into sight. The country thereabouts is lovely and rolling; great trees and gentle risings in the fields. It could be days distant from London. Suburbia has some-how by-passed it. A little village with a charming inn, clean and, for a wonder, freshly painted. A Norman church in ruins. An-other, and a later church. Some gates to large estates. Roads closely lined by hedges. Then a sudden turning, and an entrance leading to a brick house far back from the road and surrounded by undulant lawns. A stop because of the gate, which has to be swung back by hand as if it had been encountered on a farm in Virginia or Kentucky. Thereafter the house.

As the three of us drove up, a maid could be seen inside, be-capped and deep in a newspaper. In a moment she was at the door, telling us in a whisper that Mr. Shaw had not yet finished his nap.

We were shown into the garden at the back of the house where the Irrepressible Virginian, as an old friend of Mr. Shaw's, pro-ceeded uninvited to pick at random a generous armful of his flowers. The gardener, clipping his way from behind a hedge, surveyed the ravaged beds with proper bourgeois amazement.

"Don't worry," drawled the Virginian, with a gesture toward the house, "he's always writing communistic stuff. It's high time someone practiced what he preaches."

The words were freshly uttered when the Elderly Gentleman, who is seldom caught napping, emerged and started walking toward us across the lawn. At first glance he looked as pale as his beard and leaner than a soda straw. His neck was as erect as ever; his back, too, even though he swayed a bit uncertainly as he approached.

He was wearing gray knickers, gray woolen socks (especially woven for the left and right foot, according to the Virginian), a gray short coat, and a bulbous cap. When near enough for intro-ductions, I could see how much he had aged since I had met him twelve years ago.

His beard was thinned, though even now gloriously prophetic and whiter than typewriter paper before being sullied by an author. Close up, his skin looked much as if the pink and blue periods of Picasso had been jointly transferred to alabaster. His eyes were at moments frosted by age. They could, however, clear cloudlessly into the most animated nursery blue. His voice remained an instrument, in register and as used, to which he would have had to give his full approval in the distant days when he was a music critic. The resonance of his speech was as extraordinary as the glory of his English—an English in which the Irish long ago became neutral. No one could create anywhere a finer figure of a prophet than time and G.B.S. have made of Mr. Shaw.

He led us around the garden, showing us the wood he saws. The cuts were feeble, as he freely confessed, pointing out that one soon grows tired of that sort of thing. Then he took us to his doll's house of a study down at the lawn's edge; that prefabricated one-room house, which he turns by a crank so that the sun is always full upon him. It was jammed with papers, books, and a typewriter—telltale because uncovered.

"I've been writing an article," he confessed.

"But why," asked the Virginian, "when you should be resting?"

"Because"—and at this a grin from ear to ear which lifted the beard—"because I'm being paid twenty-five pounds for it."

He admitted he had just finished a book on *Everybody's Political What's What,* and (I dreaded to have him say it) was about to begin a new play.

By the time we had followed him back to the house, he had already lunged into sex, marriage, primogeniture, cattle, the English clergy, Norman architecture, and Victorian bad taste.

"Sit down, sit down," he exclaimed when we had come into the living room, which was all windows and sunlight and shadowless, and highly polished furniture and books. "No special chairs here."

Then tea was served to us—delicious tea, beautifully served—while he took a glass of hot milk. The talk continued, wobbling from subject to subject much as he had swayed in his walking. As he talked he pinkened, gathering strength with his thoughts.

His talk?

"The Navy's a strange life," he said for no apparent reason, except that I was wearing blues. "Men go into the Navy—at least, they do in this country—thinking they will enjoy it. They do enjoy it for a year. At least the stupid ones do, riding back and forth quite dully on ships. The bright ones learn they don't like it in a half year. But there's always the thought of that pension, if only they stay in. So they do stay in. They stay in and are promoted as a matter of time, if not of course.

"Gradually they become crazy. Crazier and crazier. Only the Navy has no way of distinguishing between the sane and the insane. I know this because a friend of mine once took a ship across the Bay of Biscay. Even his crew knew he was mad when he crossed and recrossed the Bay five times without ever putting in. Then they threw him in the brig. Only about five per cent of the men in the Royal Navy have the sea in their veins. These are the ones who become captains. Thereafter they are segregated on their bridges. If they are not mad before this, they go mad then. And the maddest of these become admirals. Tell your Admiral this."

With the speed, and often with the brilliance with which he hedgehops from subject to subject in the subdivisions of his prefaces, the Elderly Gentleman held forth. On Lunacharsky. On Mrs. Shaw's will. On his disappointment in the man known to the world as Uncle Jo. On his visits to the front in the last war. On General Haig. On Mrs. Patrick Campbell. On Hesketh Pearson. On Mr. Shaw—"the historic Shaw, the man of my middle years, the Shaw the world will remember," as he put it. On the movie of *Caesar and Cleopatra*. And as casually as you mention a friend seen last week, on Stanley, the Stanley of "Mr. Livingstone, I presume." "I remember Stanley telling me that only five per cent of the men under him were ever equipped to take over his command, if he had to delegate authority. That's how rare real leadership always is."

"My actuarial expectancy," said the Elderly Gentleman, sipping his hot milk, and smiling as wholeheartedly as at the best of jokes, "is three days. As a matter of fact, I may die while you are sitting here. Death has no terrors for me."

But what about the war which for the tranquil moment in the

88

midst of such good, civilized talk was as lulled as if by an armistice? What about this war, in reality so near, and the next one, God willing, so far away?

"If they are not careful at the peace conference," the Sage of Ayot St. Lawrence was saying, "there will be another war in ten or twenty years. The best guarantee of future peace is that war is no longer anything but economically ruinous. Once upon a time it used to pay. This made men unable to resist it.

"You would conquer a town, and having conquered it, you had it to take as plunder. A Wallenstein or a Marlborough would enter with his army, granting his soldiers two days' leave for rape and pillage. Even then, when order was reestablished, there was the town itself as a plum for the conqueror. But nowadays what happens? We conquer not to take but to destroy. All this bombing of Berlin would justify itself, if after it we still had a Berlin to take, as it deserves to be taken. But we don't. Instead we destroy what we might have used. And have to destroy it in order to survive."

"But is there no way in the future . . . ?"

"There would be no wars if only men read my books. And took them to heart." Then he smiled again, as gaily as if he were discussing the possible nearness of his own death. "That's silly of me, really silly. I ought to know better. They wouldn't understand."

By the visit's end, the Elderly Gentleman, so frail and mortal behind his prophet's beard, seemed tired. Slowly and unsteadily, though erect as an exclamation point, he had preceded us to the gate. As he stood there in the road while we drove off, with the breeze ballooning his cap, with the sun hallowing his beard, and an arm upraised, the saintly old Satan or, more accurately, the satanic old saint looked more alone than any man I have ever seen. He was as alone as only old age and such a mind as his can make a man.

In the preface to *Heartbreak House* he had written, "Only those who have lived through a first-rate war, not in the field, but at home, and kept their heads, can possibly understand the bit-

89

terness of Shakespeare and Swift, who both went through this experience."

We left him standing there by the green hedges of an England once again at war. We left him standing there, once again surrounded by a world of death and destruction. It was a world which must have made him feel as if all these decades during which he has preached, his millions of words have been heard only by the deaf. It was a world beset with more ills than any single mind—even his with its all-embracing inconsistencies—could hope to suggest remedies for. It was a tragic world, which tragically for him and us had passed beyond him.

In the lengthening distance he looked as if he were a revivalist about to address a meeting.

"I must preach and preach and preach," had said the character in *Too True to Be Good,* "no matter how late the hour and how short the day, no matter whether I have nothing to say."

Although there was only sunlight in the fields, one suspected that in such a world Mr. Shaw must have felt himself enveloped by a fog; the same kind of fog that enveloped the preacher in *Too True to Be Good.*

"There is left only fog," runs the stage direction there; *"impenetrable fog, but the incorrigible preacher will not be denied his peroration, which, could we only hear it distinctly, would probably run—*

"I must preach and preach and preach—no matter whether I have nothing to say or whether in some pentecostal flame of revelation the Spirit will descend upon me and inspire me with a message, the sound of which shall go out unto all lands and realize for us at last the Kingdom and the Power and the Glory for ever and ever. Amen."

Like everyone else, we were too far away. We could not hear him.

90

Chapter VII

All in One Bloom

The flowers in the London shops continued to be few and of a wintertime variety, as pale as clerks, though more dearly bought. To the florists the spring was obviously a military secret. They guarded it with as much zeal as if they shared its buds with the War Office, the Admiralty, or the Supreme Command.

There are secrets, however, which refuse to be kept. Any spring is one of these. This spring was more insistently communicative than most. Its coming was whispered at first by timid informers, then trumpeted by heralds posted everywhere. And everywhere, to people directly or indirectly concerned, it contradicted itself upon arrival, affirming and denying all in one bloom, demanding in its gentle loveliness to be recognized as spring even while its beauties muttered the most unspringlike of certainties.

London resisted it at first as cities will. But not for long. The spring, which had warmed the countryside and us on our visit to Ayot St. Lawrence, was by now nudging its way into the capital. Miles of brick and stone, of asphalt and of rubble, could not hold it back. Neither could the fumes of Army and Navy cars, of trucks and taxis, nor the hostile feet of men. Everywhere it was demanding life, and finding it.

The large parks—Green, St. James's, and Hyde—had surrendered first. Before such an underground movement they were powerless. Their allegiance had never really been in doubt. Even during the bleak winter months they gave it to the countryside. Now they went over as a matter of principle, because spring, after all, is a principle no less than a season.

To American eyes, accustomed to the browns and blacks of

winter, the grass in these London parks had always remained green. This green, paled by the sunless cold and often winter-faded into mouse gray, suddenly refreshed itself. It, too, was dipped in the spring. The great old wrinkled trees rebelled at being Arthur Rackham models. With their thousand-fingered branches they clutched at life, setting down samples of Arden and Sherwood and reminders of the Park at Windsor in the heart of a grateful city. Walking through these one almost forgot the antiaircraft guns, the searchlights, the Niessen huts, the rocket guns, and the barbed wire with which they bristled—and almost forgot what this spring meant.

The squares responded more slowly than the parks. So color-less, so tired, so man-trampled and death-accepting during the winter days, they had at first the look of casualties. Fenceless like the parks, they were scarred by ugly water tanks needed for fire fighting during the air raids. For weeks one could have sworn that they had lost the will to live.

Then one day Romeo, the barrage balloon, which for dreary months had been the only bloom in our headquarters square, ceased to blossom above leafless trees. Buds reddened on the branches far below. Some crocuses forced their way through the cinders on the roadway now used as a parking space for American Navy and Army cars. A cluster of laburnum trees brightened the gray stretches of the square with patches of soft yellow. Green leaves followed in profusion. Life was everywhere. At least in nature.

Life was also in the millions of young soldiers all over England, whose tanks now nestled close to hedges heavy with leaves, or who could guard their ammunition dumps against everything except the encroachments of the meadows. It was also in the young sailors who, when they steered their little craft back from practice landings into South Coast harbors, could see the gorse lion yellow against the new greens on the hills. It was also in the youngsters who, dispatched on missions night after night and day after day, carried their bombs across the green and yellow check-erboard of England.

Life was everywhere—meaning also across the Channel in the

The Spring Invades Eisenhower Platz

prison known as Fortress Europe. The daisies were riotous in Normandy and Brittany. Had not General Rommel told us this? According to reports, he had inspected them—yes, inspected the spring daisies—and commented on their beauty, adding how beautiful it was to think of the thousands upon thousands of mines hidden beneath them.

Never before had small flowers, cupping their heads toward light and life, cast such long shadows. These shadows crossed the oceans and penetrated the thickest walls. Beauty and ugliness, youth and oblivion, joy and sorrow, death and life had not hitherto lived in such a oneness and on such a scale.

The chill of apprehension was in the April air. Even in May one could have sworn the frost was constant. Certainly for many the days grew rarer in June.

The spring is a phenomenon occurring not only in the outside world. It also happens inside men. It quickens the blood along with the sap. It is the season of the young, when even the old feel younger. The only death it recognizes is winter's death; and this death of death it celebrates joyfully.

> *Make an eternal spring!*
> *Give life to this dark world which lieth dead.*

Although the spring in England has been sung by the world's supreme singers, the poets have no copyright on it. It does not have to be hymned in daffydowndilly terms about shepherds and shepherdesses, or greeted with a hey and a ho, and a hey nonino, to have plain men recognize it as the best, though by no means the only, pretty ring time. The greenwood tree issues its own invitations. But to what? To lie with whom? Millions of young Americans, along with millions of young Britishers, who happened to be in England this April, were asking themselves this. The question remained in their hearts when May followed and the peach trees bloomed, and the wise thrush sang each song twice over,

> *Lest you should think he never could recapture*
> *The first fine careless rapture!*

"Make an eternal spring!"

The young Americans responded to the season's rapture in their own American way. That they were young men in uniform did not prevent them from being young men in the spring. It only emphasized the fact.

They wrote even warmer letters home. They swayed with new frenzy to the rug-cutting summons of the records of Harry James and Tommy Dorsey. They listened wistfully in groups to albums of *Oklahoma!*, their eyes shining as they joined in the singing of "Oh, What a Beautiful Morning!"

They tossed baseballs in the surprised sidestreets of Mayfair. Or, before Britishers who could not have been more delighted had they been spying on Navajos performing a tribal dance, they played the game as Dodger fans should whenever they found a clear space in the parks or countryside.

They picked up their own Phyllises and Amaryllises, greeting these dames with a hopeful "Hiya, babe?" They looked the more hungrily on the uninhibited curves and postures of the pin-up girls in their lockers or on their walls; girls as unmistakably American as they were unmistakably girls, and prized the more for this because even sex has a national accent. At country dances held in stuffy town halls they amazed the natives and their slower footed English partners by teaching them how to get in the groove or by replacing the local drummers and saxophonists and donating the plasma of their own sense of rhythm to orchestras more accustomed to Sunday concerts on the green than to jive. In a thousand ways they showed they were alive and had no dislike for living.

The lovelier the spring became the more some of us applauded an invader well out of hearing upon his choice of a season. The summer has always been history's favorite time for wars and picnics. On calm seas and firm green ground and under a warm sun, troops and trippers and their equipment have always fared best.

William the Conqueror did not see it this way. When he came over from Normandy, the life seasons of spring and summer had spent themselves. It was late in September when he landed. And

October when he met Harold at Hastings. The fall was already in the air, and the winter near enough at hand for nature to be in a gravedigging mood. But the spring is different, joyously different.

The middle-aged and the young had often during these smiling weeks discussed death quite frankly. The popular notion is that men in uniform can imagine death only as something happening to everyone except themselves. This modest or immodest belief is supposed to be a blessing. It is said to fortify men as they approach danger.

Perhaps it would fortify them if only it were true. My ears and heart, however, tell me it is a lie. Each man I talked to was immodest or modest enough to feel that death might be interested in him. He did not openly avow this. He had too much pride for that. Yet he suffered from inward misgivings which would creep up on him and stab him at unexpected moments. Most of us, I know, as the moment became inevitable, began writing letters home which, though we hoped they would not serve as last letters, were felt and phrased so that they might. Oddly enough, though we could imagine our dying, none of us ever pictured himself as being wounded.

During the spring a question which interested some of us was whether it would be harder for the young to die before having really lived or for the middle-aged to forswear life, having tasted its pleasures and responsibilities. The young, needless to say, were all in favor of granting the middle-aged this particular priority. Their attitude, most naturally, was "After you, Alphonse." The middle-aged had strong arguments on their side, and would have liked to advance them with greater fervor. But they also had their doubts. The discussion, of course, filled only idle hours. No doubt it was the most academic argument known to man since the scholars of the Middle Ages had pondered how many angels could stand on the point of a needle.

Before the spring had epitomized the hope of victory and the problem of death, the bookish ones among us had talked a lot about William the Conqueror. Especially in the winter days. We had not fully appreciated then the felicity of his taste in seasons. We had seen the story of our Invasion, whenever it did come, as the great story of William in reverse, a William who was a liberator, not a conqueror.

In the many months of our guessing we had pored over the pages of a monograph on the Bayeux tapestry. We had smiled then at the horses William used as tanks. We had noted how much his early LCVP's resembled our own invasion barges. And we had laughed at the hints of radar to be found in these quaint old sketches.

In the chill months, when we went out in the Channel on maneuvers, we bookish ones had derived the pleasures of the library-reared by touching hands with the history all around us. It stirred us to think that at this point from which we were sailing Richard Coeur de Lion had set forth for the Crusades. It amused us to know that William of Orange had landed near by. It pleased us to remember that not far away the Armada had swept past; that Frobisher and Raleigh, Nelson, and even Captain Bligh had been in these same waters; waters which had halted Hitler and which Napoleon had managed to cross only as a passenger on a British man-of-war.

But as April came and went and May followed, we closed our history books without meaning to do so. The past slipped unnoticed from our consciousness. We lost our interest in what had happened to William, and cared only for what might happen to us. The spring, no doubt, with its insistence upon life brought this about; especially since the spring for all of us was the unmistakable symbol of our own nearness to history still-to-be-made.

Those of us not in the know had played hare and hounds all winter long with every possible clue we chanced upon. Though busy, the first December days had dragged. They were leisurely enough to inform us that we had time. By January and February the beat of the tom-toms, originally so deliberate, had begun to quicken. By March this beat had accelerated more compellingly than the savage drums in the *Emperor Jones*. By April it was furious and insistent. By May it had reached a full crescendo, chang-

Spring and the South Coast

ing the tempo of our hearts.

The hints? More accurately, the hints for us at our headquarters, because these hints, though bound to be different for men and women all over England in every type of service, were nonetheless unmistakable.

The world knew General Eisenhower was to be the Supreme Commander. But he was in the Mediterranean when we first heard this. Then, one sightless, fog-bound Sunday a long brown car bearing four stars on a red background crawled like a lamed beetle through the thick carpet of the fog up to Grosvenor Square. And HE stepped out. Thereafter, Supreme Headquarters Allied Expeditionary Force, more commonly known as SHAEF, became for all of us a reality.

The hints?

The maneuvers off the South Coast. Each one of these was a full, grim dress rehearsal of what was to come. Each one of these involved thousands and thousands of men and countless craft. Each one of these ran the risks of enemy attack from the air or sea. As the spring flowered, these maneuvers increased as surely as the heat does before a violent summer storm.

Other hints at our headquarters?

Admiral Kirk's already overcrowded schedule became more and more overcrowded. No day was long enough for what he and his Chief of Staff, Admiral Struble, managed to get done. Conferences with General Eisenhower, Admiral Ramsay, Admiral Stark, General Montgomery, General Bradley, General Brereton, and their staffs grew in frequency. The Admiralty's green "scrambler" phones buzzed up and down the kingdom. Admiral Hall and Admiral Wilkes came up from the South Coast more often, looking more serious each time. The Gold Braid multiplied until the beams groaned beneath it. Admiral Moon and Commodore Edgar arrived, causing those of us who passed them in the hallways to speculate upon their duties. So did Commodore Sullivan. And Admiral Deyo and Admiral Bryant.

Meanwhile scuttlebutt not only boiled but boiled over. Every mouth was a foaming caldron for it; every ear a sturdy ladle.

The lights inside the black-out curtains at Number 15 burned longer and longer into the nights. The mimeograph machines knew few undizzied moments. Yeomen pounded typewriters like woodpeckers holding a convention. The Invasion factory hummed. It was working overtime. One look at the desks of Lieutenant Bundy or Lieutenant Commander Berger, the Admiral's Military and Naval aides, made this clear. For that matter, so did one look at either of these hard-pressed young men.

The eyes of the Photo Interpreters—Lieutenants Coleman, Haas, Bear, Califf, etc.—became more and more strained as they exhausted them poring over pictures of enemy strong points through the stereoscope. The eyes of the shoreline map artists —Lieutenant Bostick and his crew—reddened as behind locked doors these men bent night and day over their drawing boards. Under the eyes of such intelligence officers as Lieutenants Cowan and Deakin, the circles darkened as the hours lengthened without mercy; and without mercy the details multiplied.

The marines subjected us to drills with our masks on in a gas-filled chamber, while Navy doctors lectured us on the horrors of mustard or lewisite gas.

All the Section Heads—Captain Mitchell, Captain Ragonnet, Captain McShane, Captain Wellings, Captain Batchelder, Colonel Jeschke, Commander Kime, Commander Bayes, Commander Robinson, and their subalterns—toiled increasingly, while mountains of official documents, marked "Top Secret," crossed the desk of Lieutenant Cragg as Flag Secretary.

Meanwhile, the Communicators labored overtime; and messages to and from Washington piled up on the dispatch board like ticker tape on Broadway after a parade. Meanwhile, too, Captain Dowling, our Staff Force Medical Officer, faced realistically the handling of the Invasion's casualties, planning mercifully, thoroughly; planning, planning, planning as everyone else was planning. In all this planning between Allies, in this snowstorm of battle plans, the Army, the Navy, and the Air Forces planned as one.

At last we heard that the *Augusta* was to be our flagship. We

101

then saw light at the long tunnel's end.

Soon thereafter, when the spring was already upon us and Commander Steere, our aerologist, was poring over his weather charts with more concentration than any gypsy has ever consulted tea leaves, we discovered that our Task Force was to be subdivided into three groups: one, the lucky and the rightly envied, to go with Admiral Kirk on his flagship; another to be hut-based for the time being in a South Coast port; the third, and smallest, to continue its much needed intelligence work in London under Lieutenant Commander Hunt.

The announcement of forward and rear echelons is always anguishing. Among military operations this severance is one of the most painful. Its casualties are wounded spirits. This is why they hurt beyond remedy. Even a flagship must float, and to float can carry only so many. Hence, the pains of the pruning; the dashed hopes, the ardent protests, the pleas to be taken along.

Moving day followed in a short time. Number 15, once so populous and busy, became overnight as empty as a college dormitory on the day after graduation. Its desks and files and maps, its treasured plans, its safes and records, were piled up under guard on the pavements out front and under guard taken southward by truck in the spring air either to the *Augusta* or the waiting huts.

The British Government had banned civilian travel to the coast. Those of us whose duties even now led us from a deserted London southward and back again understood the reason for this ban. We could not help noting the changes each time we entered the restricted area.

Daily the harbors were filling with ships. The roads were increasingly clotted with trucks and tanks, with jeeps and guns, with bulldozers and ambulances—all heading south in a telltale migration. At some points the meadows which fringed the beaches were stippled with great spreads of gravel. These shone ivory white against the coastline's billiard-table green. They were guarantees of the under-wheel dryness of the loading points, regardless of the whims of English weather. In other places ramps

102

Our Photo Interpreters at Work

made from cement blocks sloped down straight into the water as nests for hungry amphibious craft. These points, where vessels had to be loaded with the things needed last put in first, became as faultlessly methodized as the assembly belts at Willow Run.

There was a false "Alert" late in May which carried off the press, rucksack and typewriter, from London to the flowerful serenity of a small coast town. This false "Alert" was a ruse, designed to confuse the enemy. It was asked for by the British, no doubt, in the hope that as the liquor became more plentiful at the Savoy, any enemy agents who might be lurking there would naturally assume the Invasion was on.

Then there were the newspapers, in America and in England, in Germany and in France, in Switzerland and in Sweden, which daily beat the tom-toms until they were thunderous with rumors.

There were whisperings, too, within our ranks. And statements made which by themselves meant nothing but which when joined with other such statements put feathers on the arrows.

Above all, there were the faces of the GI's one passed on the hedge-lined roads of southern England. Some observers had thought these young Americans soft when they had first touched Britain. By now they were toughened, bronzed, and ready. The lines of their faces looked as if they had been sculptured by some ennobling Phidiases of the filling stations and the farmlands. Ceasing to be merely boys in uniform, these youngsters had become recruiting station posters of themselves. The spring had ripened them, too.

Also eloquent in announcing the nearness of *the* day was the Sunday—the last in May—when churches all over England were crowded and their altars bright with spring flowers.

The church to which I was drawn in London on North Audley Street turned out to be high Anglican. Empty when I arrived early, it filled with mysterious promptness. The people who swarmed there were chiefly old couples, or young women, often in black and no less often accompanied by children with cherry-pink cheeks. They prayed long and earnestly upon reaching their pews. Although they sang a Whitsunday hymn uncertainly, all of

Lt. William A. Bostick

Chow Line Forming

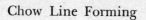

them were certainty itself when they raised their voices, clearly, beautifully, to release the words of "God Save the King."

The lesson was from Ezekiel. It had to do with the valley of bones, those dry bones which the holy man was told to prophesy would have flesh on them. And the flesh appeared, though there was still no breath in the bodies. "Prophesy that they breathe," said the Lord. And Ezekiel so prophesied. And the winds from the four corners of the earth blew; and they did breathe—these bones, first fleshless, then clothed with flesh, but needing the Lord for life.

When the time for announcements came, the minister—a grave, lean-faced, bald-headed Britisher, a Justice of the Church—looked above his horn-rimmed spectacles to say, "If news of the Invasion comes any day this week, or next, or in the coming weeks, I want you to know this church will be open that night for prayers and a choral service in honor of God's cause on the Far Shore."

Finally on the South Coast there was the King's visit to the *Augusta*. With Admiral Ramsay he had come to inspect the American Naval Forces under Admiral Kirk which alongside the British would participate in the Invasion.

Although several days of polishing and rubbing had preceded his visit, the men could not, for reasons of security, be told who was coming.

After a tour of the harbor with the Admiral on a PT boat commanded by Lieutenant Commander Bulkeley, the King stepped lightly up the gangway. Then it was that the *Augusta*'s sailors, tired from standing in the cold (because that day it was as cold as if the spring had never come), saw in the flesh a face familiar to them on coins and stamps. It was a young face drawn with fatigue; a fine face, really; sensitive, sad, and above all gentle.

The King's manner radiated controlled timidity and disciplined· shyness. He looked as if he hated being the center of so much attention. Yet his smile was so gracious and his step so agile that as a man he conquered Americans reared in sections not apt to be overenthusiastic about British kings.

As an official finale the King's visit was equaled only by the

106

His Majesty Visits the *Augusta*

arrival of the Navy-attached U.S. correspondents. What smoke is to fire and bees are to the hive, correspondents are to news. Everyone who saw these men come aboard knew that something, including the anchor, would soon be up. When they had gone south this time, the correspondents had been briefed in the southern area by Admiral Hall; and in the southeastern area by Admiral Kirk, Admiral Moon, and Commodore Edgar. Thereafter they had been sealed and taken at once to the sealed ships, upon which all of us were by then impatiently waiting.

If anyone still had doubts about the moment's being at hand, these doubts evaporated when with their staffs the Generals came aboard. First, Lieutenant General Omar N. Bradley, as commander of the First Army and second to General Eisenhower in the American Army's Chain of Command. To those of us who had been in Sicily with Admiral Kirk, General Bradley was an old friend. We had carried him there on the *Ancon*. We knew the presence of this quiet, imperturbable gentleman meant one thing—action. Next, there was Major General Ralph Royce of the 9th Air Force, fresh from the Mediterranean and the Pacific. And, lastly, Major General Laycock, Lord Louis Mountbatten's successor in Combined Operations, who came as an observer. Our forces were joined. The sea, the land, and the air were now one; eager to move, ready to strike, and shipbound.

To any lover of the sea, the mere act of being on a ship is one of the most exhilarating of life's experiences. Even in peacetime the lungs grow larger when fed upon sea air; the eyes brighten; and the horizon beckons. No ordinary ship, however, can equal in excitement the suspense aboard a vessel about to be battle-bound. It is a form of lightning which strikes the keel and travels fore and aft.

Just then the horizon was beckoning us with a Titan's urgency, while on sealed ships of every kind and size we waited for the word to go.

As the skies, until recently so blue, grayed and the Channel became choppy and chill, we on the *Augusta* forgot about the wonders of this English spring. We wanted only to get going.

Circling—

Forming Up to Move In

Across the Channel were millions of people who in their hearts had not known the spring for four appalling years. No one could blame them if they felt that even this spring—this glorious spring now turned battleship gray on the Invasion's eve—was late in coming. As always, however, it would prove worth waiting for; if only it bloomed according to our prayers and plans.

III
Action

"... O, do but think
You stand upon the rivage, and behold
A city on th' inconstant billows dancing:
For so appears this fleet majestical."

Henry V

Chapter VIII

Coming Events

We are headed for the Bay of the Seine, immediately to the east of the Cherbourg peninsula. We Americans are the Western Task Force. To the east of us will be the British or Eastern Task Force.

Dinner was over. The second and last of our Last Suppers had been downed. The great decision was by now a matter of history, although recorded history did not as yet know it. This decision had been reached hours before these words began to bark out over the *Augusta*'s Public Address system.

The harbor's entrance was far behind us. The green hills had long since disappeared. Under the gray skies of a forgotten spring we were cutting our way briskly through the gray waters of the open Channel. In a twilight, Scandinavian in its length, we were still skirting the English coast, heading for a friendly rendezvous, before a sharp turn to starboard would point us straight toward France and whatever the morrow might bring.

We, and the destroyers already with us, were not sailing alone. In the Irish Sea, through St. George's Channel, in the Bristol Channel, past Lands End, down from the Humber and the Wash, or out from behind the Isle of Wight, other vessels were moving—some four thousand of them, including ship-borne LCVP's, of all sizes and at all speeds, from harbors large and small all over Britain.

Over breakfast coffee no one could as yet read about tomorrow and the next momentous days. This casual reading had to wait until these men could make it possible by doing what they still had to do and facing the unknown which enveloped them. Even then, these particular sailors and GI's would be the last to read about the doubtful days at hand, if by then they were still reading.

The battle had not for them become, and was never to become, a matter of those newspaper maps, so clear and decisive, so easy to scrutinize or skip, on which the countless anybodies, who happen to be somebodies to themselves and to their families and friends, are replaced, along with their doubts and fears and agonies, by neat crisscross lines, tiny opposing flags, swirling arrows, and the names of hitherto unheard-of villages. Before any battle maps of Normandy could be printed, some of these men would have to engrave them with their blood.

Naturally, they were interested in their place in the scheme of things. Wouldn't you be, if, knowing the darkness was approaching, you happened to be moving forward toward enemy shores across' hostile waters? Naturally, they sought the pattern of what might be. This is different—very different—from the blueprint of what has been.

To civilians far away, even to servicemen in other theatres, the Chain of Command in a remote operation is apt, no less naturally, to be a bore. Its melancholy practice is to list the secondary actors in a performance put on where it cannot be seen. It is too technical to enjoy widespread consumption at home. America is proud of her men in uniform—ask any Congressman—but no less proud of not knowing too much about the military.

To the soldiers and sailors moving into a battle, however, the Chain of Command is a road map. Like all road maps it gains in interest when you are the person taking the trip it happens to direct. As the twilight waters of the Channel splashed our bows, there came, accordingly, over the *Augusta's* loud-speaker:

The Supreme Commander of the Allied Expeditionary Force is, as you know, General Eisenhower. The Allied Naval Com-

mander in command of both of these assaulting naval forces is Admiral Sir Bertram Ramsay. The Commander of the Eastern, or British, Task Force is Admiral Vian. The Western Task Force, of which the Augusta *is the flagship, is under the command of Admiral Kirk.*

The news here, for sailors on the *Augusta* who had grown accustomed to being overcrowded by the presence of the Flag and to whom Admiral Kirk had for some time been a familiar figure, consisted only in placing the main British Task Force in relation to our own and naming its commander. But what about the subsidiary commands? And the general plan of attack, which was sending all these men and vessels into this cold spring night, if no further?

The Western, or predominantly American, Task Force is divided into three task forces: one under Admiral Hall; another under Admiral Moon; and the third, a follow-up group to sail a little later, under Commodore Edgar. A fourth American unit, under Admiral Wilkes, Commander of Landing Craft and Bases, will remain in England until the time comes for it to move over to the far shore. Admiral Bryant is in command of the battleships; Admiral Deyo, of the destroyers.

For those of us who had watched these worthies during the spring months on their visits to London, this cleared up much. For those on the *Augusta* who time after time had piped them aboard, greeted them, or heard their comings and goings announced over the Public Address system, such a statement turned still other guesses into certainties. If you are one of the small fry, it is as interesting in the service to know who has been selected to command a military show as at home it is to learn who, if drafted, will consent to accept a political nomination.

Of the three American Task Forces, those under Admiral Hall and Admiral Moon are the assault forces. As for the Augusta, *she*

115

and the squadron of PT boats to escort her under Lieutenant Commander Bulkeley, will constitute a Control Force, which will also include destroyers and other ships. We will have wide latitude of movement.

The Eastern, or British, Task Force will carry the British Second Army and consist of three assault forces.

So much for the Chain of Naval Command, the major distribution of naval forces, and the general plan. To by-pass the intricacies of the plan, and so to simplify its many-paged minutiae, amounts to scribbling Acts I, II, III, IV, and V quite boldly on a sheet of paper and pretending to have written *Henry V*. Yet these were the plan's main points. As the twilight deepened on June 5, they were new to most of us on the *Augusta*. They had to be, for our well-being no less than that of those at home.

Geography comes next, as come it must. Invasions are not accomplished by standing still. Invaders must move to invade, even as these men on the *Augusta* were then moving to a destination they had just learned.

By now everyone everywhere must have mastered all details pertaining to the Bay of the Seine. You may have forgotten them. So much has happened since. News, especially good news, is a crop which rotates itself, plowing under what has gone before.

You must have heard these beaches described on the radio. You must have seen them in the newsreels or the public prints. With your own eyes you must have explored this bay on newspaper maps. Long ago you may even have spent a pleasant vacation on its then undamaged shores. But ours that night was not a pleasure cruise. We could not turn over the page if a sprightlier picture captured our attention on the next.

Most of the young men on these moving ships had never heard of the Bay of the Seine before or dreamed of going there—even yesterday. Some of them would never leave it. No man knew his fate that night. Neither did any of the moving ships. This is what was different for these men. Steaming in person into any un-

"We come in here, see?"

fought battle is strangely different from reading about that battle at a merciful distance when once it has been won or lost.

If you will look at the map of France (which you cannot do often enough just now), you will find that the northern shore line of France dips down into an irregular curve at Calais, where the distance between England and France is shortest in the Dover Straits.

From Calais to Cherbourg at the tip of the Cotentin peninsula to the west, the French coast line resembles the fat end of a slice of pie bitten into by a person with irregular, though prominent, teeth. In this bite our business lies; this bite which is the Bay of the Seine.

But how to get in? And at what? These are problems which the maps must leave unexplained. This is where the ink turns into blood.

You will notice that there are no ports of any size in this area; in other words, that we, as amphibians, will be performing our proper amphibious duties, moving from ship to shore and also from shore to shore.

"Amphibious" is by now a household word. It crept gradually into the public consciousness. A few years back it belonged to zoology, not warfare. At first it was used cautiously as an adjective to describe landing operations or types of equipment. Then the Amphibious Forces, like Hester Prynne, won their capital "A," though in their case for assault, not surrender.

Amphibious operations are as old as the Trojan War; as old, in fact, as the need of getting troops by water from one beach to another. They have become as pronounced a characteristic of this war as trenches were of the last. Special tactics have been developed for them; and all those ugly ducklings of the Navy— the LST's, the LCI(L)'s, the LCT's, the LCVP's, etc.—have come proudly into their own.

118

In amphibious warfare the fighting is not from ship to ship. The aim is not to surprise or engage the enemy at sea, but to surprise him by landing on his beaches. Enemy beaches are amphibious ports.

The French coast line subject to our joint assault is a stretch roughly of forty-eight miles. These forty-eight miles will not be under complete attack. Some ten miles of coast will, for example, separate us in the Western Task Force from the British, or Eastern, Task Force. Our own two assault forces under Admiral Hall and Admiral Moon will have as their objectives beaches likewise separated by another ten miles.

The facts that the beaches were not contiguous and that each beach presented its own problems in terrain, defense, and attack were points the full importance of which most of us did not grasp that evening, when southern England remained in sight and German-held France was still an unkept appointment with a stranger.

Admiral Hall's ·Task Force is the eastern of the two American assault forces. Admiral Moon's Task Force will attack a beach to the westward. On or back of both beaches are small villages.

The names of these villages were to be found on the maps. And the maps were to be found on the walls of the steel hut used by the Intelligence Section. But tomorrow, and this was hard to realize, Colleville and Pouppéville would no longer be black dots on paper. They would be real villages under fire and before our eyes.

Of the two beaches Admiral Moon's is in the flatter country. It is said to consist mainly of sand dunes or masonry walls. Behind it, however, are drainage canals which the Germans have blocked up, thus flooding the adjacent country. Although the land is reported to be drying in this area, and the three roads inland are

119

said to be clearing, the other roads still have some water on them, and the ground near by is extremely wet.

No land seems so distant or mysterious as one that is enemy-held. Even when the enemy is only around the next hill, that hill steps out of nature. In the broad sunlight it becomes more drenched in shadows than the darkest dungeon. The enemy's presence turns noon into midnight. Every bush and tree, every farmhouse and hedge, loses its country innocence. The drabbest description of an enemy position is exciting when the enemy is still there, and the job at hand is to see that he does not remain there.

In the area which Admiral Hall's Task Force will attack, the beaches are backed by sharp cliffs, presenting a pocket-sized edition of the White Cliffs of Dover. Four valleys cut through this section, and the land rises inland from nine to one hundred and fifteen feet. It is in this area that the main German counter-attack against the Americans is expected.

Our job is to land our men before Germans can mass theirs. Our assets in the initial attack are our air supremacy and the strength and accuracy of our naval guns.

What follows was good news; sweet music to each one of us at a moment when sweet music was welcome. There is safety in numbers. Comfort, too—especially for Americans. We like buildings, bank accounts, books, and movies to be bigger than big. We like them biggest. This fondness for size was Paul Bunyan's bequest to us. That night we were more overjoyed than ever before to discover he had had so much to give us.

The naval forces with which we sail represent the greatest ever assembled in history. Counting all American and British craft with us, we will have some 2400 craft in the Western Task Force

120

Welcoming Committee—

French Cliffs and German Mines and Obstacles before D-day

alone, of which about 1300 are ships of, or above, the size of LCT's.

To be more specific, when we confront those German-held beaches tomorrow, our Western Task Force will have with it three American battleships—the Arkansas, *the* Texas, *and the* Nevada; *three American cruisers—the* Tuscaloosa, *the* Quincy, *and the* Augusta; *thirty-two destroyers; eighteen patrol craft; two French cruisers; one big-gunned booming British monitor; and five British cruisers—the* Hawkins, *the* Belona, *the* Glasgow, *the* Black Prince, *and the* Enterprise.

If you are not Navy-minded or unless you have someone at sea, the names of naval vessels may leave you as cold as the roll call of the Roman phalanxes in Gibbon. To sailors, however, ships are very much alive. To sailors, ship names mean what hotel names mean to traveling salesmen or what the labels of fashionable dressmakers mean to women. Sailors go further. They think nothing of calling the grimmest, most death-giving mountains of gray steel by pet names.

The faces of the boys in the Pilot House that evening brightened at the mere mention of the *Texas,* the *Tuscaloosa,* or the *Nevada.*

"The good old *Texie!* I served on her onct."

"Say, I got a buddy on the *Tuscy.*"

"The *Nevada?* Sunk at Pearl Harbor and now here. Kee-rist, that's sumpin!"

And *something* the *Nevada's* presence really was; an ironic reminder of how the war had changed; a Phoenix of the deep; a symbol of our Navy once lost, now resurrected and indestructible.

The three battle wagons with us were what in the swift race of armaments are lovingly known as old tubs. But their venerability was to prove no drawback. They were not going to be called upon to outrun the enemy. The needs for great speed were slight in an area too crowded for constant maneuverability. These ships

122

carried the big guns. That was enough. More than enough as it turned out, because the big guns were to do the trick.

A major feature of the operation will be our Allied Air Forces. For months our Air Forces have been attacking enemy gun positions, roads, and bridges. They have been at it again today and will be again tonight.

At the moment, the overcast skies were planeless. As yet, they had not come out from either shore. Spotters at every level on the masts, spotters on every moving ship were looking for them. They come quickly, when they do come, those death-bearing dots on the horizon. Almost between breaths these dots swell into planes. Then they are dots again. Each man that evening stole glances at the sky. Only peacetime skies can be ignored. Mr. Chamberlain was never as much concerned with his umbrella as we were with ours.

Between midnight and H-hour tomorrow, some 3000 Allied planes should have done their final preparatory work—planes, heavy and light, bombers and fighters. During tomorrow's daylight, at least 6000 of our planes of all kinds should be in the air. At times it is said that three layers of planes will be flying over us or near us at once. A sight—a sound—none of us is apt to forget. Tonight at about midnight our air-borne troops in planes and gliders will fly over Admiral Moon's beaches. They will come in such numbers that their passing will take three hours.

"Kee-rist!" said one of the sailors in the Pilot House. The ten of them, huddled there in the smelly air, grinned from ear to ear.

We come in vast numbers on the sea and in the air. We come carrying with us a huge army. Air-borne troops will precede us in large. force. With Admiral Hall will be the 5th Corps under General Gerow; with Admiral Moon will be the 7th Corps under

123

General Collins, both of which Corps are part of the First Army commanded by Lieutenant General Bradley, now with us on the Augusta.

So much for us. Praises be that there was so much to us. But what about *them?* What could we expect from *them* in the coming hours of darkness and as the dawn broke, when every revolution of our propellers was bringing us nearer to a coast which they had made theirs?

It would be the wildest understatement to suggest that we will not be opposed.

The heavy remaining units of the German fleet consist of two pocket battleships, two old battleships, two heavy cruisers, and four light cruisers. Although it is improbable that these ships, if they do come out, will be able to evade the protecting cover force supplied both Task Forces by the Royal Navy, an attempt might be made in desperation to employ them.

The philosophers say, "Know thyself." In warfare this is not enough. You must also know the enemy; know him as well as you know yourself. You must know his strength, his mind, so far as it is possible to read it. Certainly his whereabouts. Even the old lady looking under the bed for a burglar realizes this.

What does seem likely—in fact, inevitable—is that we shall meet with opposition from German E-boats, torpedo boats of the Eblings class, and some sixty reequipped expendable enemy small craft. The Germans have for some time been experimenting with midget submarines and various forms of "human torpedoes." Cherbourg, at the tip of the peninsula, is a populous E-boat base. Then, of course, U-boats can be expected to appear.

In warfare you do not have to be Clausewitz to know that you must face the facts. The enemy are the facts.

124

It seems no less ridiculous to assume that the Luftwaffe, which for some strange reason has left us comparatively unmolested in English waters, will not try to make up for lost time off the French coast.

Then there will be mines, enough of them to keep our mine sweepers and demolition squads more than busy. And underwater obstacles of various uninviting kinds. And on the beaches strong points, pillboxes, and barbed wire.

The faces of the sailors in the Pilot House were grave. Why not? The business ahead of us was more than that.

Remember, we are moving into a heavily defended area teeming with gun emplacements; the worst of which, if one can find encouragement in this, have a range of 32,000 yards.

Translate 32,000 yards into passenger miles, and the result is roughly eighteen; much too long a distance to have begun worrying in peacetime about baggage and customs, or even language.

We face what may well turn out to be the longest General Quarters in naval history. Even as we face the greatest invasion of them all and one of those moments which change history.

We go with the blessings of our superiors.

"You are about to embark upon the Great Crusade, toward which we have striven these many months," General Eisenhower had said in a message addressed to soldiers, sailors, and airmen of the Allied Expeditionary Force. "The hopes and prayers of liberty-loving people everywhere are with you."

"I count on every man," Admiral Ramsay had written, "to do his utmost to ensure the success of this great enterprise which is the climax of the European War." In his Order of the Day addressed to the soldiers of the First Army, General Bradley had said, "The future of the war, in fact, the future of our country,

125

depends on the success of this operation. . . . It must succeed and, with God's help, it will succeed."

Finally, under the heading of "Coming Events," Admiral Kirk addressed this message "To All Hands" in the Western Task Force:

"We of the Western Naval Task Force are going to land the American Army in France.

"From battleships to landing craft ours is, in the main, an American Force. Beside us will be a mainly British Force, landing the British and Canadian troops. Overhead will fly the Allied Expeditionary Air Force. We all have the same mission—to smash our way onto the beaches and through the coastal defenses, into the heart of the enemy's fortress.

"In two ways the coming battle differs from any that we have undertaken before: it demands more seamanship and more fighting. We must operate in the waters of the English Channel and the French coast, in strong currents and twenty-foot tides. We must destroy an enemy defensive system which has been four years in the making, and our mission is one against which the enemy will throw his whole remaining strength.

"These are not beaches held by an apathetic foe or defended by hasty fortifications. These are prepared positions, held by Germans who have learned from their past failures. They have coastal batteries and mine fields; they have bombers and E-boats. They will try to use them all. We are getting into a fight.

"But it is not we who have to fear the outcome. As the Germans have learned from failure, we have learned from success. To this battle we bring our tested methods, with many new weapons, and overwhelming strength. Tides and currents present a challenge which, forewarned, we know how to meet. And it will take more than the last convulsive effort of the beaten 'master race' to match the fighting spirit of the American Navy. It is the enemy who is afraid.

"In this force there are battleships, cruisers, and destroyers. There are hundreds of landing ships and craft, scores of patrol and escort vessels, dozens of special assault craft. Every man in

126

Before—

Air View of the Beaches

his every ship has his job. And these tens of thousands of men and jobs add up to one task only—to land and support and supply and reinforce the finest Army ever sent into battle by the United States. In that task we shall not fail. I await with confidence the further proof, in this the greatest battle of them all, that American sailors are seamen and fighting men second to none.

"A. G. Kirk."

It was still gray outside. The sky, the Channel waves, and the *Augusta* were almost one in color. But it was growing darker. A fairly stiff wind, a measure of our motion, was blowing in through an open porthole in the Pilot House when I reached the last page of my broadcast. It caused the page to flutter in my hand. By now we had met up with the friendly vessels we had followed the English coast to join and were heading out into the Channel. The span of a short night separated us from a destination we knew and from a dawn and day we had yet to know.

In these hours of testing, which will, which must, lead to triumph, may I remind you of three lines from Shakespeare?

> *Therefore, my lords, omit no happy hour*
> *Which may give furth'rance to our expedition*
> *For we have now no thought in us but France.*

Good luck!

Chapter IX

The Moon Lies Fair

At 10:30 the call to General Quarters comes. It tumbles out of the *Augusta*'s loud-speakers. It floods the darkened passage-ways, the wardrooms, and the cabins. There is no stopping the rapid risings and fallings of its

Ta-ta-ta-ta
Ta-ta-ta-ta
Taa-taa-taa.

And no possibility of not responding to its summons. Of all Navy calls this one is the most irresistible. It is jubilant, jaunty, and lighthearted; nervous only in the energy with which it sends men scurrying to their Battle Stations.

Wisely it avoids the solemnity of a solemn moment. The cascade of its notes is almost a dance. It is as merry a statement of "the great defy" as mortal ears can hear. It is youth for which it bugles, youth's quick footsteps for which its half notes are designed.

"Come and get it," it sings gaily of danger, barely suppressing a smile. "Come on the double." And youth answers with its feet, as young dancers should, scraping out a carmagnole on the steel decks or pounding a drum roll of acceptance on the iron ladders which lead to duty. Even older feet recapture something of their youth when obeying this call.

Because of it, the sleepiest ship springs into wakefulness. It turns a flophouse into a traffic jam. Men thickened by their life belts, men with their heads withdrawn turtle-wise under their bulky helmets, darting men unrecognizable in the red oases of

129

light created by battle lamps burning sullenly below decks—they all start running when this call comes. They continue running with the insistence with which an alarm clock strikes. They jostle. They collide. They shove. From all directions they race to get where they belong.

Tonight they run on a ship stripped to the white bone for action. Everything is battle-ready, ready for the trouble which may come at any moment. All fire hazards have long since been disposed of. The cabins are barer than cells. Desks are closed; photographs and books stowed inside them. Razors, toothbrushes, soap, etc., have all been jammed in the medicine cabinets above the washstands. Pillows have vanished. Stiff covers, shiny with fireproofing, encase the bedding. In some cabins all electric lights except one have been removed to avoid breakage when our big guns go.

The heads are as waterless as deserts. The passageways around the funnel-like barbette have been cleared of the cots which choked them. Sleep, always the first battle casualty, has plainly walked the plank on the *Augusta*. The hatches are closed; the watertight doors shut. The *Augusta* is now subdivided irrevocably into those unyielding, prisonlike compartments below decks which arouse individual misgivings though they guarantee group safety.

Minor precautions are taken along with major ones. The long tables in the wardroom are stripped; the chairs roped together. The tiny black airplane models which used to sway above us, attacking us as we attacked the chow, have disappeared. Except for an electric toaster, some pots placed on an electric burner where hot coffee can always be had, and some thick white cups and saucers (often chipped), the galleys are idle.

We are even readier for action than we have been during all these weeks when, to unprofessional eyes, the *Augusta* has seemed readiness itself. This means more than it may appear to mean, because at all times fighting ships are nothing if not frank. They do not go in for dissembling. Their every line confesses what their business is. If their sleeves are always rolled up, it is be-

The *Nevada* Opens Up

cause their pride in their biceps is unashamed.

They are gladiators who know how to fight with every weapon except a smile. Grace they have no less than haughtiness; infinite majesty, too; and a self-confidence so innocent of doubts that it reassures each man they carry. They look and move as if it never occurred to them that anything could damage them. This is part of their strength no less than of their frowning, tight-lipped beauty.

Another source of strength is ours tonight. We share it with every moving vessel. The finest naval blueprints do not include it. Only approaching danger can evoke it. It is a present given unexpectedly by the enemy. It is that strongest cement known among men—what Agnes Smedley once described as the bond of possible death.

Make no mistake about it, the bond which is ours tonight is an extraordinary bond. Good belly laughs, good drinking evenings, bull sessions unedited and endless, poker games or golf, trips taken into or out of the woods, college years which keep regurgitating, indiscretions discreetly guarded, shared hobbies, interwoven hopes, business adventures, overlapping tastes, respecting minds toughened by friendly conflict, peacetime causes jointly championed or opposed, spirits gay, trustful, and at ease with one another, or (for the lazy) sheer propinquity—are these the roots which nourish most ordinary friendships between men?

Potent and pleasant as they are, they do not create that final sense of comradeship which exists between uniformed men who in each other's company have faced death. Among old school ties this one is the most binding. The fraternity it represents is classless, raceless, rankless. It is as democratic as its founder. And surely as a democrat Death knows no equals. Let him approach a large group of men; and their knowledge of his nearness exerts a fine, free, liberating influence on individuals made mean or small by safety. Indeed, it is one of the blessings of that sub-hell known as war, and one of man's major tragedies, that a crisis is required to make men rise.

All of our energies are mobilized tonight for one thing—sur-

132

vival, which under these circumstances is only a synonym for tomorrow's success. This means that the energy required to feed even our normal dislikes is sapped. Unless they crack pitiably as individuals, men so challenged as a group grow in stature as their danger grows. Not forever. Not, really, any longer than their danger lasts. Even the gods tired of living on Olympus. And we, as heaven and our families know, are anything but gods. We are only small men struggling to rise to that low altitude known as the crisis level. But always, if only we survive, we will have in our hearts a very special feeling for those who were with us during the testing. Yes, even for those we do not like and who heartily dislike us.

On the *Augusta* tonight this battle comradeship is in full bloom. For those of the Flag it blossomed first and unforgettably on the *Ancon* off Scoglitti in Sicily. Although it faded then, as it will fade again, it never died completely, any more than this time it will languish utterly if everything goes as we hope; in other words, if we are lucky. It has been ripening during all these months of waiting. Each London raid had revived it; each maneuver quickened it. It is pleasant to encounter it once more.

It is pleasant and as sustaining as that ruthless black coffee which is the Navy's nectar and of which most of us have drunk deep tonight. Not that we need coffee to keep us awake. The chances of dozing are nonexistent. Still, we do gulp down the black corrosive stuff—as a matter of habit, and because it is comforting to have something warm under our life belts.

Later—much later—we learn that a colored boy on one of the LCI (L)'s pushing toward France across the Channel's choppy waves approached his young skipper tonight with a request. The request was made at a time when all of us had heard that pills to cure seasickness had been distributed among sailors and soldiers.

"Skipper, can Ah have one of dose pills?" the colored boy drawled.

"Why, Sam, everyone knows you're the best sailor on this ship.

You've never been seasick yet. Why on earth do you want one of those seasickness pills?"

"No, suh, Skipper, you got me wrong. Ah don't want no seasickness pill. Ah wants one of dose Brave pills."

As we clambered up the ladders tonight and pushed aside the stiff double row of canvas flaps shielding any of our lights within from enemy eyes, all of us, I'll wager, would have gulped down whole bottles of those Brave pills, if only Captain Dowling or the *Augusta*'s doctors had had them to distribute.

On the way into battle most men wonder if they will be afraid —and are afraid they will be. No man knows how he will behave under fire until he has been under fire. Then he is never quite certain as to what he will do next time. There is always the humiliating possibility that he won't take it the way·he wants to in the presence of his fellows. That is where pride comes in— a bit of ammunition not officially recognized by the Bureau of Ordnance.

The Admiral's bridge on the *Augusta* is below the Captain's in that series of dwindling platforms which ring the foremast like bits of meat on a skewer held erect. It leads not merely a double but a various life, this bridge. It is at once the Signal Bridge, and the Admiral's, and more. Since its wings have been clipped while at home after the *Augusta*'s return from Casablanca, it has shrunken uncomfortably. Considering all the intricate work it must do, the nerve center that it is to the entire American operation, and the many officers and sailors who must crowd it (even when their numbers have been reduced to the strictest essentials), it is far from ideal. For Flag purposes it is what an ice cube is to a polar bear.

In tonight's darkness it is not unlike Times Square in a blackout. At first the men on it are no more than three-dimensional shadows. It almost takes Braille to make them out.

This fellow you bump into with laughing apologies proves to be either Lieutenant Olsen or Lieutenant Reynolds, two fumiferous inseparables who even by daylight would be hard to distinguish with their cigars. Or Lieutenant Bundy or Lieu-

134

tenant Commander Berger. General Royce or a signalman. A sailor headstrung with a walkie-talkie, or Captain Ragonnet. Hanson Baldwin of *The New York Times,* a gunner, or Commander Bays. Major Hanson or Captain Heath. Lieutenant Commander Griggs or Jack Jarrell of INS. Lieutenant Rice or General Bradley. Admiral Struble, a yeoman, or Admiral Kirk. Then, after a few stumbling minutes in the cold air, carrots declare their tardy dividends, and night vision and cat's-eyes come into their own.

An impending battle is heady stuff. No other bad champagne sends such bubbles bouncing through the veins. It produces an inflation of the spirit. In the horrible suspense of waiting for what at any moment may come at you from anywhere out of the darkness, one fights first against an insane desire to laugh at almost anything. The good old-fashioned, school-day giggles lurk around black corners.

No doubt it is the nervousness men feel which makes some of them giddy. It overstimulates them. Perhaps this is why not a few of us tonight could swear we must have been dieting on Benzedrine.

Certainly quite a number of us are charged with a strange mixture of calm and exuberance, both of which are unnatural. The exuberance is the same forced gaiety which in a hospital can possess the most Caspar Milquetoast of patients when being wheeled to the table. The calm is the hush which seizes you when in the small black hours your senses awaken you to whisper that someone may be on the far side of your door, trying to get in. Giddy or silent, all of us are conscious of the tension of these minutes made of rubber; these watchful minutes which stretch out into hours.

In the armed services you must have patience. Waiting is a large portion of each day's business. This waiting, however, is of a new variety. It lacks the usual resignation. It is anything but uniformed Yogi. A bow could not be more taut.

From the forward lookout to the marines in their open gun tubs on the fantail, all eyes topside are turned on the waters and the skies. On the Admiral's bridge and on the Captain's bridge

135

above it, constant crossings from port to starboard and back again are made by men leaving a wake of half-finished, muted sentences behind them. These men seem pulled to this side or to that by the binoculars glued to their eyes.

As midnight approaches—and passes—all ears are trained for the promised roar of our planes. The clouds are low. And as dark as black sheep everywhere, except at their edges which are grayed by the moonlight above. Although planes are reported constantly, and from time to time the roar of a few motors does push toward us through the clouds, we are denied the sight of that great layer of air protection which we had longed to see. These planes have come over—they are coming over—in droves to the east of us.

In such darkness it is impossible to make out the ships near us, except at those moments when the moon threatens to break through. Even so, we wonder about those four thousand vessels moving with us across these waters. We wonder particularly about those ships upon which we have friends. We wonder what these friends are doing, saying, thinking. We trust that all is well with them. We wish we were together.

In these hushed moments we also think of home. Often. Gratefully. Longingly. In sudden half thoughts. In full minutes of delicious and deliberate reveries. Or in terms of visual images which appear unsummoned and in sound-tracked technicolor before our eyes, between us and the water or the sky that we are scanning.

We wonder, too, about the enemy. About his Luftwaffe. And when it will come swooping toward us through the clouds. About his shore batteries when the dawn will bring us before them as targets. About his movable guns mounted on railroad cars. Most especially, about the six largest German guns on Pointe du Hoe, off which Admiral Kirk has chosen our anchorage.

We also wonder about those fearsome underwater obstacles, and about our sailors and soldiers who in so short a living time must go through them. We wonder, too, about the enemy's mines through which we may be passing. They might be anywhere;

136

sea-sown some time back or plane-dropped this very evening. We thank God for our mine sweepers forging valiantly ahead of us, like lawn mowers clearing paths in a field of tall weeds. They are cutting those needed, mine-swept passages upon which depend not only our safe approach but the whole elaborate design of our battle plan. Wondering in this fashion, we sneak below from time to time for some more cups of strong black coffee.

Jottings made in the darkness may give some notion of those events which chart our interests during what for all of us is the shortest long night and the longest short night we have lived. At 4:15 a piece of land is sighted. Land for us has only one easy, challenging, and by now welcome meaning. Two minutes later a group of destroyers under Admiral Deyo is reported going into Admiral Moon's beach.

At 4:26 a column of ships is said to be off our starboard beam. More land is sighted at 4:35. This, needless to say, is reported to the men below decks. In the next few minutes we are slowing down to five knots, though because of this our hearts are accelerating. In the blackness now and then some tiny lights on the water can be seen, no larger than the tail torches of lightning bugs. To see them requires straining. From the decks of a cruiser they could be flecks of phosphorus in the Gulf Stream. They are hooded, exposed only to those approaching from our direction. Rumor says little British craft have placed them at intervals to mark the course for our young pilots.

Things are coming to a head. At last the climax is at hand. We are near—which means that *they* are near. The moments have almost overtaken us which have occasioned all this planning, this mass migration, this labor and this worry in the States, and this drilling and this homesickness abroad.

These moments must already have been faced by the paratroopers and the glider-borne soldiers. Doubtless they have by now been dropped or landed behind enemy lines. Under the mask of this darkness, in which we still find the illusion of safety, they must have had their rendezvous with danger. In strange fields,

137

crouching behind hedges or walls, caught in trees or swamps, they must be in action.

Meanwhile, metallic voices drone over the intership phones. They are voices from Mars with nail files for palates. They are inhuman in their tinniness as they scrape out reports studded with code names; as they question, answer, or command. They seem to come abruptly from nowhere. Just as suddenly they are swallowed up in the night air.

At 4:42 a flare is visible off to port, one of the many flares we are to see, though there is still no fire from the beaches. Mercifully, too, none of those enemy searchlights has reached out for us, stabbing the vanishing darkness to expose us and explore us without pity, as the searchlights did off Sicily. Furthermore, none of those horrendous, self-perpetuating chandelier flares of the Germans is hung above us, as a necklace of them was off Scoglitti, turning night into day and us into so many seagoing Godivas. For this we are duly thankful.

At 4:55 a burning plane off our starboard bow tumbles into the sea like a torch being extinguished in a tub. Whose plane it is, we do not know. We guess it must be ours, because *their* planes have not as yet come out and because of the ack-ack suddenly pelting the sky from the shore.

Gradually the long short night retreats. The darkness lifts slowly, imperceptibly. It rises like a thick velvet drop in a theatre to disclose a gauze curtain, misty and mysterious, behind which is a half-lighted set that requires time to perceive. Slowly in the dawn's faint blue-grays the ships near us reveal themselves.

The wind is somewhat brisker than is healthy for small landing craft. But they are in the water, heavily loaded; loaded no doubt with seasickness, too; and waiting. Near us a host of LCI's stand by, also heavily loaded, and ready to nose into shore. The *Arkansas* and the *Glasgow* are in position. The old *Texas,* looking strangely like a Gothic nightmare in the half-light, is ahead of us. As far as the eye can see, there are ships, countless ships, more ships than one would have guessed there were in the world, ships of every kind, ships which multiply as the light increases.

Lt. Dwight Shepler

D-day

Miraculously, in spite of their different speeds and sizes and the youth of most of their navigators, these vessels and craft have found their way in the night through the crowded Channel and mine-swept courses to their appointed places. Now, as neatly ordered for the most part as chessmen on a board and as seemingly serene as if this were just one more, though far greater, maneuver off Slapton Sands, they confront beaches which have just stolen into view.

Our engines, which have stopped at 5:22, now move us in nearer. Some distant explosions can be heard behind the emerging wall of cliffs. Patches of red light scar the sky ahead. Admiral Kirk, Admiral Struble, General Bradley, and General Royce never take their eyes off the scene before them. When they speak to one another, or give orders, they do so calmly, quietly, without turning their heads and usually without lowering their glasses.

We are within *their* range. H-hour is scheduled for 5:50. H-hour is almost here. The naval bombardment is to last thereafter for forty minutes. Between what the air has done and the Navy's guns will do, the bastions of Fortress Europe should be in a receptive mood for the Army when the little boats go into these heavily defended beaches. If only . . . if only . . .

It is almost time to stuff the ears with bits of cotton. When the big guns go, they thunder like near-by echoes of the Judgment Day. They assault not only the enemy's strong points but the eardrums of those aboard the ships which reel under them. Accordingly, I go to the Pilot House to the fore of the Admiral's bridge. My job is to attempt to describe the scene for those so stationed that they cannot see it; to tell them of H-hour and the approaching bombardment; and to prepare them for the firing of our own big guns.

As always, the Pilot House is crowded. As always, it has the smell of a flophouse built underground. An inexhaustible pot of hot coffee, darker than the blackest socks, is the magnet which usually draws the sailors here for a few snatched seconds of rest and refreshment. This early morning the sudden transients and

140

Sea, Land, and Air

*Admiral Kirk, General Bradley, Admiral Struble, and General Royce
Follow the Invasion from the Augusta's Bridge on D-day*

those on duty here have more than black coffee to lure them.

The portholes are open. Through them a breeze is blowing which would air any other room except this rounded passageway of steel, which has gone so long unventilated that it resists airing even now. Through the round frames of these portholes, France is a picture coming into focus. The grays of the cliffs are gradually bleaching; the grays, where there are trees and grass, deepening into daylight green. Pointe du Hoe, the objective of the Rangers, now takes shape. Remembering the six enemy guns reported on its summit, it has for us in the Pilot House the fascination of a boa constrictor.

George Wheeler of NBC is perched on a stool at the central porthole with a mike in his hand. He is to record history for us on the *Augusta,* as George Hicks of the Blue Network and Charles Collingwood of CBS are to record it in their battle broadcasts from other vessels. All three are using the Navy's sound track boxes, capable of providing their descriptions with a background of the authentic action noises.

Fred Frutchey is Wheeler's fine technician. Both are watching our forward gun turrets as they revolve directly in front of and below us, slowly swinging their giant fingers into position. The men on the *Augusta* know that the sound track film of this recording will be sent back by dispatch boat to London, there to be broadcast to America. It pleases them to think that their families back home will thus be in on the Invasion too, and to realize that our salvos will indeed be shots heard round the world.

The distant rumble of guns ceases to be distant. Some shore batteries open up with what sound like very deliberate beats on a deep-voiced tom-tom. The *Texas* answers as quickly as an echo. She answers furiously with enough fire to avenge the Alamo. Great clouds of smoke pour out of her; flames spill from her like oranges from a broken crate. She is ablaze with her own fire; indeed, she seems struck merely because of the frenzy of her striking.

We do not have to be told that H-hour is at hand. On all sides it announces itself with a booming and banging, a banging and

Battle for the Beaches

booming. There never has been such a wholesale Knocking at the Gate. Battleships, cruisers, destroyers—they all let go. The entrance march is played by an orchestra composed entirely of kettledrums.

A church steeple comes into view like a toy in a shop window, while tracers burn their way into the sky, chasing one another implacably in their rise and fall.

We have stopped now. At 6:10 we prepare to fire. In the Pilot House we see our guns pause ominously; pause and point. Having found their target, they halt and follow it like a diviner's hazel wand over water. Then we wait. We wait, like all people waiting to hear a pointed gun fired. We wait. And just when we are holding our twice-inhaled breath, the *Augusta* quivers beneath us.

The sound invades our ears. Even the cotton cannot hold it back. It roars at well-timed intervals, like a volcano trained to choral action. Each time the roar comes fore or aft, the *Augusta* lurches slightly, as from a ground swell of noise. Then she rights herself with a dowager's dignity. The smoke ahead of us is heavy whenever the forward turrets have their say. Thereafter this smoke vanishes, like the flames which beckoned it into wide rings, even as the smoke evaporates, screening a conjurer's trick.

We have scarcely concluded our first salvos; and the hullabaloo all around us is going full blast, when the rocket ships near by release their quivers of fire toward the beaches. With a swish accompanying each burning tier, as if an abscessed cloud were being punctured, they whistle their flaming discharge in the air. London, with its rocket guns which dislodge the innards of those who follow their sibilant exhalations, has accustomed us to these screeching missiles. So have the maneuvers.

Then we start firing again. Once again we are unchallenged.

We have fired fifty rounds. Or is it fifty-five? I do not know. I cannot pretend to count them. I know only that nothing answers; that mercifully and incredibly we have been talking very loud in the ears of deaf-mutes.

144

After—

Land View of the Demolished Obstacles

At 6:45 we move again. Like an orator who has spoken his piece, we leave the platform, heading for the transport area.

The *Ancon* is near us. Her familiar outlines, for those of us who were aboard her off Sicily, unleash memories of other sleepless nights and other attacks. The water all around us is alive with little boats moving in. Although the *Texas* is still firing, it is quieter now. Much quieter. The group barrage is over. Single battleships and destroyers continue their individual duels with shore batteries, still lobbing them in. The main bombardment now lasts only as an unsilenced echo in our ears. What a few moments ago was a mob brawl has shrunk to fierce personal scuffles.

The Navy guns, aided by spotters, have evidently done their clean, precise, devastating work. We gather from the general silence that they must have neutralized most of the shore batteries. They have gone where our planes could not go. They have reached in under the ten-foot blocks of cement which hood the enemy strong points and offer them the protection of submarine pens. Against these they have obviously scored Annie Oakley after Annie Oakley. The proof of their accuracy is the comparative silence and a coast line puffing out sporadic bursts of smoke. Evidently the Navy's gunners have exceeded the elder Tell's talent for apple-cleaving.

Although our Air Force has performed a major service brilliantly, disrupting enemy communications, bringing in paratroopers and gliders, and throwing the Germans off the scent for the deceptive swath of its bombings so late as last night, it has been able in many cases to scratch no more than the surface of these strong points. On one fearless low-altitude flight after another, however, our Air Force has swooped down on these beaches, photographing the snaggle-toothed underwater obstacles, the barriers, the mines, and the gun emplacements. These photographs, when developed in London, have for months in advance of our coming been pored over by our photo interpreters. Their findings have served as Gideons to our gunners during the naval bombardment. As it turns out, our P.I.'s have performed miracles in locating the targets just silenced by our Navy guns.

146

Bull's-Eye for the Navy

A German Strong Point after the Naval Bombardment

The calm out here cheers us and perplexes us. We know that the regatta aspects of our position are deceptive. At these very moments, when we cannot believe our fortune, the little boats, out of our unaided sight, are scraping against the land's edge. The first waves are facing annihilation; the beachmasters are at work; and those landings are being made which are the sole point of this limitless armada.

Seen through binoculars on the large ships, the shore is an anthill in turmoil. The death cries do not reach us. The falling bodies we do not see. The first desperate dash through the water is beyond our vision. The first contacts with the barriers and obstacles we can only guess at. The first, and all-important, hand-to-hand test of arms we do not share. We do not even hear the sulphurous stammering of the machine guns. The initial confusion is not ours. We know only this unholy and disquieting calm. And learn that the destroyer *Corry* has been sunk. And thank our stars that so far we have been missed.

We have seen two—or is it three?—American planes shot down by now. For us, however, the conflict and the wreckage on the beaches reduces itself to sudden bass rumblings from the shore, and thick clouds of smoke which announce that ships or landing craft have been hit.

But the Americans *have* landed! The British, too! They *are* on those impregnable beaches. They have crossed those barricades and faced those machine guns and mortars. The stream of empty LCVP's and of small craft pouring out from Admiral Hall's beach assures us of this, as we nibble at our K-rations, watching, wondering, doing both feverishly.

The sky is dotted every now and then with our planes. The sea we have had almost unchallenged. The air is ours, also unchallenged by *them*. The challenging beaches are now ours, too.

At first we are happy in this knowledge and this calm. The fateful dent has been made in Hitler's armor; the fortress is thrown open. Somewhat to our surprise, we are alive and afloat. Our joy, however, which from the first has been incredulous, is short-lived.

148

Hopeful Gunners

We feel let down. Cheated, almost. Depressed by the sense of anticlimax which invades us.

By the time some patches of blue have broken through the gray sky and a strong wind is roughening the seas, our elation fades. The most optimistic of us becomes suspicious. Where is the Luftwaffe? What about the railroad guns? The E-boats? The U-boats? The mines? What about all the things that might and should have happened, and which we have been expecting momentarily? Isn't this quiet reception a Nazi trap? Our nightmare has proved to be only a dream. Certainly it is too good to be true.

Some life belts, some empty vehicles, and some tires floating out from the beaches during the day persuade us we are wrong. Inshore it has not been easy. There has been plenty of ground opposition. Plenty of heroism, too. As yet we do not know the casualties. No one does.

We have so far missed what they are facing. It is they who are taking it today. But tonight? Tonight will probably be our turn. For this we must wait. And wonder. Meanwhile all that matters is that the invaders have invaded, and that the Invasion has got off to a better start than we ever dared to hope for.

Chapter X

Darkness Visible

For the first six days that we lay off Normandy, time was for us a quilt and the nights so many dark patches cut in almost identical patterns from the same rough piece of cloth. The sunlit hours were varied in their colors; the short hours of darkness were not. After each day's interruption they recommenced not as continuations of themselves but as reprints.

The number of nightly "Alerts," the hour of the attacks made on us, the amount of stuff *they* dropped near by, the duration of the fireworks which each night made confetti of the black sky, and the casualties suffered by our barrage balloons, our ships, our own aircraft, or the enemy's—these did alter somewhat between each setting and rising of the sun. Not much. Never enough to persuade us, whether we came in late or early, that the feature film was not the same.

By day the *Augusta* was apt to shuttle back and forth between the two American beaches. She would drop her anchor here or there in either area much as a visiting supervisor deposits his hat first in one classroom, then another. As flagship she was busy. Her directorial duties were manifold. The communicators could testify to this. So could the men listening to the voice circuits. The Duty Officers realized it to their sorrow. The Section Heads knew it. The Chief of Staff would have smilingly admitted it. Even the young gunners, anxious only to be firing their guns at all times, were forced resentfully to concede this.

These daylight crossings and recrossings of the *Augusta* enabled Admiral Kirk to check upon the needs and progress of the operation. They likewise carried General Bradley where he had occasion to go.

151

But from these sallies, we, the small fry, also learned much. Passing through lanes of ships, with a forest of other masts and funnels to seaward, none of us could avoid the Invasion's enormity. The armada revealed to us by the dawn of D-day was only one Task Force or a fraction of the ships off France. The English and Canadian forces we did not see. We guessed, however, at their size by the huge explosions which thundered to the east by day and by the great swaying canopy of tracer bullets which hung over them at intervals each night.

From the air the vessels in Admiral Moon's and Admiral Hall's beaches must have resembled highway traffic late on a Sunday afternoon when gas was unrationed. With this difference —there was no joy riding here.

Daily we saw these vessels disgorge; feeding, supplying, adding to the men and machines already landed. Either they nosed directly into shore through waters still splashed at moments by enemy shells, or, on bulging rhino ferries and small craft riding low, they moved in their brown tanks and trucks and guns. These small craft were also loaded down with men in brown; young men, bronzed, grim, and silent, who eyed the nearing beaches intently with looks easier to understand than forget.

Daily we watched the sky, now gray and overcast, now blue and sun-filled, as Allied planes crossed us in coveys, winging their way in or out, the bombers heavy and pregnant on the way in, light and delivered on the way out. Their black and white markings were clearly, encouragingly visible.

Or we heard the *Texas*, still filibustering in her fury. And the *Arkansas*, the *Nevada*, the *Tuscaloosa*, or the *Quincy*, as the sound trailed the hot smoke rolling out of them when they struck to support our forces pushing inland. Or we saw destroyers elbowing straight up against the cliffs, their guns pointed almost skyward, to shoot it out in furious duels with an as yet unsilenced German battery above them.

We saw planes shot down. We saw the sky over or near the beaches suddenly funneled again and again with smoke. And heard Gargantuan blastings inland as they rumbled out toward

Wounded Rangers Taken Aboard the *Texas*

us. But, unless we got ashore, the dreamlike quality of our days persisted.

We were in the midst of a crucial combat area. The fate of more than Europe was being fought for within what was at first the range of our binoculars. Yet by day, when shipbound, we small fry on the *Augusta* felt strangely isolated; out of touch; ashamed to be so static when under the cover of our guns so many men were facing death. If the truth must be known, often we were downright bored.

Apparently our isolation was not shared by those far away. Whenever they followed Big Ben on the air, the BBC broadcasters, who did not suffer from the privileged disadvantage of being present, seemed to know precisely what was happening all around us in the Channel, in the air, and on the beaches. We envied them their full-throated knowledge. And resented it. It irritated us, perhaps unfairly, to have them describe for us from miles away in easy, over-purple, unexcited English the show being given inside the very theatre in whose lobby we were compelled to wait, peeping at the stage through a half-opened door, eager to get in.

For our own knowledge of what was happening all around us during these suspended days we had to rely upon the confused reports brought by our binoculars; upon the reverberations which slowly and significantly retreated inland; upon the descriptions of those who had been ashore; upon the summaries culled from the dispatches which dropped down on the *Augusta* like pieces from an infinite jigsaw puzzle; and upon the changing battle lines we eyed eagerly each morning and evening on the maps in the Joint Operations shed.

Although, to the enemy's misery and the Army's comfort, Navy guns were in close touch with the shore throughout D-day and the days thereafter, we, as individuals, were not. We had no way of being unless we went into the beaches.

We were anything but unsympathetic to what the men ashore had undergone and were undergoing. The truth is we could not keep our interests anchored at sea, though our business kept us there. Our shells, however, could go where we could not and see what our duty prevented us from seeing. The mile or so which separated us from the beaches, though nothing to our guns, was for us a wall over the high top of which we could not hope to look, unless we put it behind us.

Our guns had a greater range than our imaginations. Among war's horrors is the brutal fact that its horrors cannot be imagined. They must be seen, felt, experienced, and survived to be known or believed. Even then they resist full communication. The most gruesome photographs only seem to tell everything. They would tell more if they recorded sounds, human no less than mechanical. And tell still more if the camera, which can reach into the interior of battered buildings, could extend its reach to include the inner, unspeaking consciousness of the children, women, and men war bruises at the moment of their agony.

We did our poor best on the ship to imagine what was happening inland. We fretted because our best was not good enough by day to draw us closer in.

My own deepest disappointment, once the barrage was over, was with D-day itself. It was a disappointment born of surprise, relief, fatigue, and of natural forebodings. Remembering the long months of the build-up, the suspense of the approach, and what we dreaded, expected—even looked forward to—as we neared France, it was hard to believe we were alive, afloat, and unhit, with both our forces and the Luftwaffe ashore. In my broadcast to the ship's company late that afternoon, I tried to state what a few of us small fry felt when I said that "So far—so far, mind you, and speaking only for the *Augusta*—D-day itself has, since the thrills of the approach and the bombardment, been almost as quiet and almost as much of a letdown as a bachelor cruise on the Albany night boat."

This, of course, was before the first of those nights off Normandy had overtaken and included us. Although these nights came near to being changeless in their pattern, they changed everything for us soon after each sunset. They were as active as the days were becalmed. For those who had not been ashore, they possessed a reality the sunlit hours could not claim.

In spite of our wanderings by day, each night found us anchored off the hills and cliffs of Admiral Hall's beach. Little by little the daily routine of the ship had reasserted itself. It had emerged slowly, timidly, from the battle routine. Sleep, when not nonexistent, was still something to be snatched at in quick, short sudden gulps, the way a turtle bolts down his specks of food.

But K-rations had given way to sandwiches, and sandwiches to hot soup and sandwiches, and hot soup and sandwiches to meals self-served. Men off duty looked skyward less often when they crossed the well deck and heard the roar of planes. They felt increasingly safe in assuming that only their own planes would be flying above them in the sunlight.

Of course, there were mines. Plenty of them. They cost us ships. Their planting was one of the reasons for each night's violence. But unless you were a lookout, you could no more worry about mines at all times than you could stand taut throughout the day waiting for a German shell to come out and reach you. Anyway, we had faith in our mine sweepers. So we went about our business by day almost as relaxed as we had been in our South Coast harbor.

The nights were different. They never surrendered to the day's illusion of calm. The dark hours remained aggressively faithful to their battle routine. They adhered so strictly to this routine that in time not only the night's incessant false alarms and mammoth tracer-bullet displays but even their really serious threats came as close to being monotonous as danger can. Which is closer than one might think, though still very far from being the same thing.

Since any of these first six nights could serve as stand-ins for the others, it seems fair to choose at random and let the night of June 7 speak for them all.

It was just after eleven when Captain Wellings came into the Junior Officers' Wardroom and over coffee casually remarked that we would have an air attack within the next fifteen minutes.

The Captain's reason? The moon; the newly risen full moon,

156

A Rhino Ferry, Heavily Laden

bright and glorious. Some of us had watched it rise, our thoughts being removed from battle because of it.

The moon, when fullish and bright and serenade-provoking, and when just looming over the horizon, is a favorite naval marker for German bombers. It serves its military, no less than its amorous, purposes. It, too, is a double-faced coin like war itself, which on one side is all gallantry, sacrifice, patriotism, adventure, giving, selflessness, bigness, and increased decencies; and on the other, all horror, death, maiming, foolishness, waste, cruelty, selfishness, ambition, boredom, grabbing, littleness, misery, and despicable destruction.

Ships cast long shadows during those first two hours after dark when the new fullish moon has climbed skyward to no more than twenty or forty degrees. These shadows enlarge the target for an airman. As a target the thousands of ships off France were already large enough. History knew no equal in size to the target we had presented the surprised shore batteries. We had got them before they could get us. The enemy's planes should have an easier time. The element of surprise had certainly vanished. It would be hard for anyone who flew over us not to hit something, even if he had never been up in a plane before. Moreover, when German pilots rush in toward the moon, on the shadow side of a ship, enemy planes are hard to spot against the sky.

Captain Wellings argued smilingly that the two hours after nightfall and before dawn would prove eventful. They did.

Prior to this discussion over coffee, a sprightly gun duel between the ships and the shore had occurred off our stern toward Port en Bessin. The red and white tracers had skimmed across the sky to meet one another. Explosions off our bow port had followed, creating bright poppies in the gathering darkness. Just before eleven what looked, sounded, and burned like an ammunition dump was ignited by a bomb dropped in the Colleville area.

These first excitements were only side shows to what Captain Wellings had rightly prophesied would next be seen under the Big Tent.

Within the quarter-hour named by the Captain and while the

158

coffee was still hot and bitter on our tongues, enemy planes could be heard churning above the stretch of clouds now over the armada, though not shielding it from the moonlight.

The whir of motors—including enemy motors—was the only match needed to set off the fireworks. Nightly these displays inundated the heavens, with and without reason, at intervals unguessable but frequent.

Then the gunners on the near-by LST's and transports had themselves a field day. Let one gun go, and guns followed almost everywhere. Let one itchy finger release a shell, and a forest of itchy fingers followed suit, often whether the plane was ours or *theirs,* visible or not, this time and every time, each night for the first five nights whenever the contagion spread. Thereafter the contagion was halted, and halted decisively.

The drone of ack-ack was everywhere. The sky filled with tracers; tracers seen at a distance to stern; tracers arching slowly into the clouds to starboard; tracers hanging a red umbrella directly over us. They quivered and spread like the light-broken darkness in your eyeballs when you press your closed lids hard with rotating fingers.

When possible, we followed each of the crisscross paths these tracers cut, wondering if at this or that path's end was a plane which would cross ours. We watched the fountains of light as they erupted on the horizon, swept in toward us, over us, and past us. Meanwhile the drone of enemy planes died away. The colored fountains were gradually turned down. A barrage balloon, an innocent bystander, swirled in flames into the flak-speckled waters.

A lull followed. More coffee. Some talk in the wardroom with men glad to get their helmets off. Some talk, too, at another table with Colonel Jeschke and Fairman Cowan on the dangers of lateral fire aimed at a plane supposedly flying low. Some jokes and friendly insults with Lieutenants Bevin or Milliken, Commander Marbet, Lieutenant Commander Graham, or Hunter, Parsons, and Williams, the marine orderlies. A nap during which the ears remained awake. For an alarm clock, some gunfire close by.

159

A quick grab for helmets. Another scampering up the ladders, past men sleeping in the dim passageways. A push through the cool blackness of the Admiral's bridge. Some hurried questions asked at the rails of Berger, Olsen, Captain Ragonnet, Leonard May, Jack Perry or Commander Robinson. Or, on Captain Jones's uncovered bridge above, some more questions asked of Jack Jarrell, Commodore Sullivan, Hanson Baldwin, Commander Phares, or Captain Jones. And a pause waiting for what would come next that must be reported to the men below.

The waiting for something to come toward you in the darkness is always strange, even if it does not come. It is then that the breath unconsciously is held longer and inhaled less deeply. It is then that all glasses, all helmeted heads, all naked eyes, all upturned faces, white in the night, are apt to move in unison. It is then that comments exchanged between those waiting grow shorter, dwindling into a mere "There!" "Look!" "Gee!" "Close," or, best of all, "They got it!" It is then, too, that one realizes how different the official report is from the individual response. On the log it matters whether it is 0318 or 0426 when a Ju 88 comes over. But to the man not keeping the log the exact time is an irrelevance. He knows that if they get him, he won't be able to tell the time anyway. If they don't get him, the time doesn't matter much. At least not to him. All that matters then is the memory of the approaching plane, and the fact that it missed and passed out of sight. When it has passed, words stretch themselves out into sentences once more.

At that moment we were waiting in some suspense. On the bridge the rumor had spread, as rumors will, that the Germans were attacking us with radio-controlled bombs. The sky was once again a close red and white polka dot of tracers. Mysterious whizzings were heard. The procession of light and noise again moved above us, back and forth, disorderly and angry, but also beautiful; possessed of the same kind of beauty as the aurora borealis. If anything, this giant demonstration was larger, more flaming, than the first.

During one of these tracer-and-flak shows on the night of the seventh—I can't remember which—some flak banged against one of our forward turrets. But at least only a few of those German chandelier flares dripped from the sky to leave us as exposed as a South Sea woman in the *National Geographic*. It was during the second of these antiaircraft displays that an enemy plane burst into flames and tumbled seaward like a burning haystack.

Another lull, welcome and incredible; a short silence more dramatic by contrast than the noise which had preceded it. A lull which was soon interrupted by intermittent explosions on the beaches and sudden, faraway eruptions of tracers or flares. They came like periods at the end of very long sentences, punctuating the unexpected silence. All at once, heavy firing was heard out toward the screen; and a cluster of flares lighted the sky in that direction, two betrayals of activity left unexplained until we heard that some E-boats were said to be approaching. Again we waited, squinting to scan the dark water for black streaks racing furiously. But we did not see them. They did not get in to us.

Except for sporadic explosions on the beaches, the night's excitements now began to taper off. Then more coffee in the wardroom. More talk. More coffee. And an hour or so of unbroken sleep before the gun crews were again being summoned over the Public Address system to report topside.

This time when we joggled up the ladders, the commotion we found was of no more than a popgun variety. The sky was graying; the ships all around were taking shape. So was the beach. The sun soon followed. With its coming, the boys in the gun tubs began to stretch and loll. Most of us breathed deeply, with a recess lightness in our hearts. Sunrise meant the yawns could be released which had been stifled by the nights that for a few of us were almost sleepless. It heralded a quiet day aboard. It reestablished that calm which the darkness had destroyed; that calm which would have been comforting had not proofs of action on the near-by beaches told us it was only a delusion.

For us afloat, each daylight had the same meaning; each night an almost identical turbulence. Each night produced the same mammoth displays of flak and fireworks. Each night took the same blazing toll of barrage balloons, and a lesser one of planes. Each night clotted the intership phones with "Alerts," warnings, and alarms. Each night vibrated with enough disturbances to justify from four to fourteen brief reports and reassurances over the Public Address system to the men below.

Each night the Germans sent up no more than thirty or forty planes over the whole Invasion area. Each night we heard the whir of the motors of at least one enemy aircraft overhead. Once one of these stitched the water with bombs just astern of us and between us and the near-by *Achenar*. Usually, however, the Germans were less interested in bombing us than they were in peppering the swept channels of the Bay of the Seine with mines. Every day and night these mines made all ship movements dangerous, and often found their victims. And almost every night during the first week, because of bombs or mines, Commodore Sullivan, our salvage expert, would dash out on a PT boat into the darkness on sudden calls to investigate a stricken ship.

One morning he came back gray and shaken, veteran though he is at such sea tragedies. He had looked upon death plain; death wholesale, too. He had looked upon that scrambling, messy death which is all the more ghoulish when encountered in the ruins of a ship's tidiness. He had seen men, once neat, self-possessed, homesick, hopeful and proud, reduced to arms, fingers, legs, intestines, and raw chunks of meat scattered beyond claiming against a crumpled bulkhead. Though no new sight to him, he was shaken by what he saw, which was hideously beyond not only salvage but identification.

We in the Navy have, as a rule, the best of war. We see superb guns shooting with marvelous accuracy at distant targets. The human cost of the hits does not come within our vision. Ours is usually the panoramic, not the close-up, view. The target for our gunners is a problem in mathematics which they solve brilliantly.

If we are doomed to die, we die quickly. That is that. The quicker the better, if death it must be. The horror of this instantaneous extinction the dying do not know. This is a horror which

162

Our Wounded Carried onto an LST

lies in the eyes of the beholder. We share it with all the services. We have no monopoly on it.

Even if death is our number, we approach it in cleanliness, with our companions, and in some comfort. We approach it as a unit, fighting not on strange soil but from a terrain we know intimately. The towns we bombard are clusters of small houses too far away for their inhabitants to be seen. Our battle is against units and machines, not individuals. We do not have to push forward alone in the darkness into single combat with an enemy who may be hiding behind any tree or wall. The snipers waiting for us are mines and planes and shore batteries. Their only concern with us is as a ship, a whole ship.

Our larger vessels may appear to be sitting ducks and bomb bait. Their very size may spread us the wider as targets. Yet so long as we remain afloat the entity of steel of which we are a part strengthens us with its own sense of strength.

We live and die in a fellowship of men who have no other choice than to be fatalists. Should death overtake us, it would find us somewhat less alone than, in the final sense, death and life are bound to find all men.

Unless we stop eating, we eat well or well enough. If we are wounded, our sick bays are at hand. If ill-fated, we go with a merciful suddenness or are saved by others of our kind. We do not become a part of the grime of muddy fields or slump down in the gullies off lonely country lanes. The sea swallows us up, which is a clean way out. It removes us from the range of gapers. It grants us this final dignity.

In the Army it is different. Sailors take their chances. Their high courage can be of the highest, Heaven knows. To defy the sea is something, even in peacetime. To defy both the sea and the enemy at once, especially when they can be one, is still more. Even so, in the Army it is different. It requires a different kind of stamina, a different kind of courage. It is the harder, the more relentless, of the two services if for no other reason than that the infantryman does not stand on his ship. So often he stands alone. Comfortable living does not exist for the soldier on the move.

Ships Everywhere

The bombardment which he faces lasts not for a battle but for a campaign. The country he must make his own is the enemy's, and this at bayonet's length.

We who had seen the Army pouring into Sicily or been with it in the cold of the Apennines around Cassino knew this. We had only to go ashore now to realize it again; to realize, also, how deceptive was the illusion of calm which by day we felt off Normandy.

Chapter XI

The Varying Shore

The beaches were different. Even from one another. They were as different as our contour maps, our reconnaissance photographs, and our Intelligence Officers said they would be. If the short distance separating us from them by day was a frontier between two worlds, the narrow estuary which divided the one American beach from the other could have been a gulf. Even when seen from the sea they confessed these differences. Their profiles could not have been more unlike.

Admiral Hall's beach to the east was a stretch either of red-brown and green Virginia hills or of venerable gray cliffs rising abruptly one hundred feet from the water. Admiral Moon's coast line to the west was sandy and flat. The one was formidable, inaccessible, bristling with natural defiance; the other, at first glance, friendly, hospitable, acquiescent. The former frowned like a tired old *maréchal* of France, baton in hand; the latter smiled like a lazy bather. Admiral Hall's beach recalled the Palisades channeling the lower Hudson above New York; Admiral Moon's the sand dunes on which during peaceful summers anyone would have gladly relaxed at Atlantic City, on Long Island, or Martha's Vineyard. General Wolfe would have felt at home scaling the first: King Canute confronting the waves from the second.

If from the sea the one beach seemed to say "Yes," the other "No," this was nature's truth, though from a military point of view merely a mirage. Dissimilar as their features were, on June 6 both beaches boasted the same limited vocabulary. Both were prepared to roar an identical "No!" and to roar it in unison, even if in different tones and in vain.

167

Both stretches of coast had to be approached through the same murderous welter of mines and underwater obstacles; barriers which by wise choice the tide of H-hour left exposed. Both beaches thundered their "No's" up to this point in the same voice. Beyond it their negatives were spoken with varying power. On shore the resistance proved to be not only as different as the two terrains, but coincided ironically with the contrasted character of the two beaches. The stronger enemy resistance came from nature's more resistant coast line: the weaker from the friendlier beach. No one could have foretold this. It was a surprise with which the Germans parried what for them must have been the very genuine surprise of the exact places chosen for our landings.

Although Admiral Moon's sand dunes took to mechanized warfare as hospitably as they had once given themselves over to bathers, their heavy defenses were, as it turned out, manned by an inexperienced Home Guard unit. The wooded hills and especially the steep cliffs on Admiral Hall's beach offered ideal locations for pill boxes and gun emplacements. Always quick to borrow, the Germans here took nature's hint and improved upon it. Worse than this, on June 6 they just happened to have one of their stronger divisions—the 352nd—on maneuvers in this area.

With the world as company, we on the *Augusta* waited anxiously for reports of the daily progress ashore. We watched the lines slowly deepen on the maps in the Joint Operations hut. We saw markings questioned on the great question mark represented by the Allied beaches change to indications of positions strongly held. And we small fry fretted. We fretted at being so near to decisive events and yet so far from them; at being on a ship contributing so vitally to the turn of these events and yet finding ourselves physically isolated from the land action. Our one desire was to get ashore; our one regret that our cruiser was not a giant DUKW.

For the first two days we listened for those rumblings which would announce that the Germans had launched their expected counterattack. We wondered if by any catastrophic mischance the thin, though deepening, lines on the beaches would, or could,

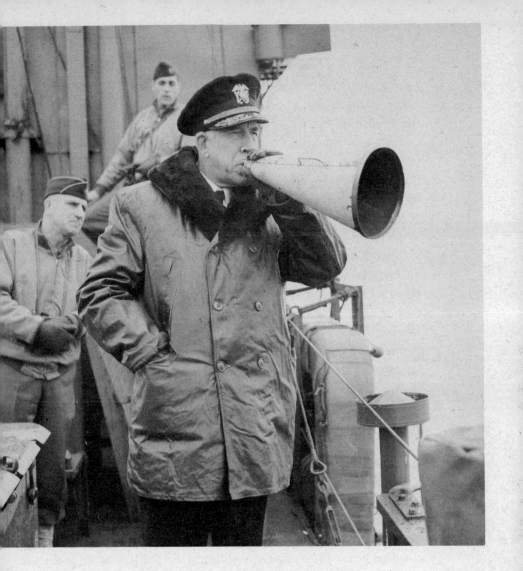

Rear Admiral John Lesslie Hall Jr., USN

be pushed back into the sea.

We knew the success of the initial landings was by no means the final test. We knew that the practice of the Germans was to guard their coasts, where the lines of defense are longest, with middling troops, and to place their best forces inland at key points on a shorter line from which they could be rushed to reinforce whatever beach area may have been attacked. We knew also that men had got ashore at Dieppe, and remained ashore at Anzio. We wanted no Dieppes or Anzios here.

There were bad moments at the outset in certain sectors where, even from the sea, what looked as if it could become a Dieppe, bettered the next day to look as if it could become an Anzio, before finally betraying the unconfused signs of conquest, smooth-flowing in its massed strength. These moments were due to the presence of that crack German division and the fiercer resistance encountered on the more difficult terrain. They were also due to the loss in these sectors, at the very start, of some Navy personnel trained in the job of bringing order out of beach confusion. If rumors had not informed us of these bad moments, the lines on the maps would have done so where, here or there, they hugged the shore without moving, remaining perilously close to the sea.

The general plan for the operation following D-day we lesser ones knew well enough. We knew, for example, that our Air Force, having accomplished its preliminary work of softening up the beaches, was to supply a constant cover. It was to down the Luftwaffe if it threatened to come up. It was to attack German positions and supplies behind the lines. It was to report and rout any massings of enemy troops. It was also to fly the more urgent of our wounded back to England from air strips established near the beaches.

From our maps and briefings we knew that our Army on its push inland was to consolidate our two very different beachheads, even while preparing a sweep to the west and south, designed to cut off the whole of the Cotentin peninsula.

The Navy's share in these proceedings was likewise clear

170

Keep 'Em Rolling

enough. Admiral Kirk had described it as landing, supporting, supplying, and reinforcing our Army. Whether we moved or remained at anchor, with our big guns ready on request to blast any Panzer division threatening our forces inland, we had only to look at the crowded waters all around us to see how fully these arduous duties were being carried out—how fully and how incessantly.

Even so, each little landing craft or stately LST, each DUKW or floating tank, each rhino ferry or PT boat that passed us, heading beachward, only increased our impatience to follow it in. By D-day's afternoon we had grown restive at knowing the general plan only in general, when robbed of its human particulars. We grew restive because we knew this plan as an idea, not an experience; in our heads, not in our nerves. We knew it in the neatness of its logic as a wise, all-covering abstraction. But we knew it without the confusions and hazards bound to be so vital a part both of its realization and reality.

Like everyone else, we knew that battles are neat only in plans or on maps. They are neat only when dehumanized on paper. They are neat only when the men who fight them are omitted, along with their fears and hesitances, their fatal or fortunate reflexes, their single acts of foolishness or courage. They are neat only when each forward-pushing inch of individual agony has been absorbed into miles of group movement; when one is talking big about the big objectives—the towns taken—and has forgotten about the fields or roads that must be fought over leading to these towns, and all the stone walls crossing these fields or lining these roads which must first be captured or passed at the cost of ignored deaths. Battles are as neat as plans, including the GI's individual plans for the future, only when they are not fought.

Quite naturally, when the major action had shifted to the land, all of us longed to go ashore, including, of course and most emphatically, the correspondents aboard. One of the ironies of amphibious warfare is how quickly the Navy's share in a successful landing is forgotten. The more excellent the Navy's job,

172

Alexander P. Russo

War Comes to Vierville-sur-Mer

the sooner the Army gets ashore; and the sooner the story follows it there. When once the Army is on enemy soil, everyone's first interest, including the Navy's, is its progress inland. Considering the new nature of the conflict there and what the Army faces every foot of the way, this is inevitable and fair. In the melodrama of battles the enemy is the villain. His presence is the plot's fascination; his annihilation its point.

It was General Bradley who, by inviting the correspondents on the *Augusta* to go in with him, made it possible for a few of us to look on the other side—the land side—of the Invasion picture. With the Admiral's permission, we accompanied General Bradley on three of the all-day visits he made ashore before he set up his headquarters on land on D plus four, thereby taking over automatically the Invasion's command in the American areas from Admiral Kirk. For my own inclusions on these visits I thank my daily broadcasts to the ship's company. I went in merely as the men's walking delegate to report to them as usual on what was happening that they could not see but which vitally concerned them. A great deal was.

It was soon after breakfast on D plus two that, as shepherded by Major Hanson, we preceded General Bradley down the rope ladder on the *Augusta*'s port side into a bouncing landing craft and headed for the wooded hills on Admiral Hall's beach to the east of the gray cliffs.

When, shortly before H-hour, France had come into focus through the frames of the portholes in the Pilot House, the mere sight of her had giddied our imaginations. The Germans, not France, had then been our concern. Even they could not rob us entirely of our excitement at seeing the French coast.

In wartime, invaded countries belong not to their own people but to the armies that have overrun them. The enemy's presence makes an enemy of the friendliest country. France was an enemy when we first saw her. She was an enemy as we approached her. She was to remain an enemy to our Army wherever German forces remained in control. Even for us at sea, the France that was French—the eternal France—came fully into our consciousness

174

only after the German guns had been silenced. She became German again by night.

To all of us the sight of France had meant the testing was at hand—the testing with Germany, significantly enough. To some of us, however, the French coast had awakened memories unrelated to this or any war as we kept looking at it during the lulls of the first two days.

Regardless of how they may feel about the French, all men have a special feeling for France. At least, they do if they have known her. The Germans, so long envious of her in spite of their professed contempt, share this feeling.

To most who have traveled there, France is as much a song as she is a country. Her years of darkness cannot hide her light. Her vices, which include her politics, are only the dark flowers she has developed because of being overcivilized. They are the price she has had to pay for her high virtues, and for the delight and drama of her contrasts.

We thought of these contrasts as by day we stood off her shores. To some of us, France was both Voltaire and Mistinguette, Proust and her peasant Joan, Robespierre and Rabelais. She was a Jacobin wearing a faded court dress. She was at once the tarnished gilt of her old palaces and the liberty she had bled for at her barricades. She was as famous for her bordellos as for her Bonaparte. She was the frugality of her bourgeois, the sharpness of her shopkeepers, the liquid precision of her language, the stained glass in her churches, the loveliness of her boulevards, and the unreality of her governments during the tragic years of the hiatus. So great was her gift for light that the wonder is she did not invent electricity. Perhaps she would have done so if in their fight against darkness her best minds had not always got along so brilliantly without it.

For two days some of us had looked at her coast line, remembering her, between explosions ashore, for the greatness of her paintings and the frankness of her post cards. The fame of her courtesans, we recalled, had rivaled that of her cardinals. We thought of her, above all, as a land of laughter and violence, of

175

beauty and reason, where the fruits of the Sorbonne and those of the vineyards had been equally prized, and where even the cooks were artists. We grieved, both for France and for those young tourists in khaki now swarming on her beaches, when we realized that, should they live until the beaches led to Paris, these men would not know on this trip the delights of France. For their sake no less than for hers, they would be duty-bound to subtract from her beauties. For them she was first and foremost a battleground.

Even by the morning of D plus two, we had not grown accustomed to the thought of having France so close at hand. To approach her in a landing craft; to see her so that the greens on her shore line became first a swirl of trees, then single trees with individual leaves shadowed by the sunlight; to see her so that the men on her beaches who had been insects through our binoculars became not only men but Americans moving, as the British and Canadians were moving to the east, on French soil, held by Germans only two days before, was to be awake in a blissful dream. It was to confuse the hot dust lifting from the beaches with dark clouds at last lifting. It was to realize that the landings in Africa, in Sicily, at Salerno, and Anzio had finally reached their great crescendo—and explanation—in Normandy.

The nearer we came to the beaches the less we thought about France, and the more we thought about what was going on ahead of us; about the Germans, and hence about ourselves. An enemy shell, lobbed in over the hills, raising a cloud on the land near by, was a sharp reminder of present business.

The beaches throbbed with activity. They were all bustle and traffic, pushing and hustle, crisscrossing and shoving, and mainly life. They hummed with a song of their own. It was an odd music made up from the backfires of huge trucks, the shout of voices, the scrape of feet, the grinding of brakes, the giant grunts and groans of bulldozers breaking their way through the landscape, and the scrunching wheels of DUKW's as they grabbed on to the gravel near the shore to lift them from the water. It was

176

Freight Yard on the Sand

broken by gunfire, and by the sound of mines being destroyed inland.

Plainly we were newly arrived in this area, and our arrival had been costly. Debris was strewn across the sand where the German barriers had been destroyed. Debris lapped against the coast line in the water. Broached landing craft or the skeletons of wrecked vessels sprawled against the shore. An LST, scorched as if forgotten in an oven, was near us, with its cargo of tanks burned paintless and blistered, with the brown blankets of its men charred into little chips the size of cornflakes. Its sole survivor was a pair of freshly polished tan shoes, belonging to an officer. They were untouched, placed neatly side by side, waiting patiently to be used.

The sands were littered with stuffs; stuffs being added to by boats newly arrived; stuffs subtracted from by returning trucks; stuffs that just sprawled in the sun and waited. At some points the beaches had the strewn look of circus grounds, when everything is spread out before the Big Tent goes up. Only these beaches were getting ready for more than one circus, however mammoth. They were preparing to hold what in reality was The Biggest Show on Earth.

The beaches were a freight yard in the sand, a freight yard without trains or tracks. On them the backlogs of an expedition were spread out. They housed a frontier city being born all at once; man-cleared and man-made but mechanized, with guns and tanks for its vigilantes, with bulldozers for its axmen, with jeeps for its broncos, with trucks and DUKW's for its covered wagons, with its labor in uniform, with foxholes and slit trenches for its residences, and barbed wire for its fences. The roads of this settlement were being laid by Seabees, and order was being established by Beach Battalions and the Army even while traffic groaned up the near-by hills and inland.

The harborless beaches were struggling to become a port: a major port, fed by more ships than most ports have ever emptied in their harbors at once. Then there was the traffic, moving laterally across the stretches of sand in front of the hills, grunting

178

Farewell to the Navy

The Army Discards Its Life Belts

up the hills, with one vehicle following another as closely as coaches on a train. At the sides of these improvised and dusty roads marched an endless file of infantry. GI's spilling from the little boats and wading into shore in numbers so prodigally fertile that they made the Trojan horse a barren amateur. GI's resting on the beaches for a tired moment, chewing on their K-rations. GI's in limitless lines moving up the hills, silhouetted against the sky like the peasant force of Russia in a Soviet movie. GI's and trucks on their way in, already passing captured Nazis being marched out. And all this under occasional fire.

Everywhere along the beaches were dumps, resembling Indian burial mounds, where incoming GI's had shed their life belts. Not all of their life belts had been abandoned in these piles. Singly or in heaps, they fringed the roads for miles inland, an American edition of the poplars.

Brown and crumpled, these discarded life belts resembled faded *leis*. They marked more than the lightening of a GI's load, whenever he had had the time to think about the weight he was carrying. They marked his farewell to the Navy. They were monuments to that phase of his adventure. Wherever they were found, "for those in peril on the sea" had become "for those in peril on the land." There are no life belts ashore.

180

Chapter XII

Where War Has Been

After we had waded in from our landing craft and scrambled halfway up a hill, breathless in the attempt to keep pace with General Bradley, he had turned to us and said, "Gentlemen, I'll be going back to the *Augusta* at about five this afternoon. Meet me here at that time. Meanwhile you can come along with me or be on your own. That's up to you. I'm going to hitchhike."

General Bradley uses the language with exactitude. When he said hitchhike, hitchhike was what he meant. He is the simplest of gentlemen. His weapon of command is understatement. He makes the role of general the more important by underplaying it. He goes in for none of the tawdrier dramatics with which military authority can exhibit itself. No flourishings of side arms, no yodelings at those who cannot answer back, no bullying, and no swagger. Just the unchallengeable authority, imperceptibly exerted, of a good, patient man who is a master at his job and genuinely cares for his men.

No official car was waiting for him. He stood by the roadside, a tall, slim figure, with the thumb of his right hand jerking inland, surveying the unbroken stream of jeeps, DUKW's, and trucks which passed. In his dark eyes was that look of hope which brightens the eyes of all hitchhikers.

A driver would suddenly notice the three stars on the General's helmet or recognize his face. A jeep would come to a sudden halt, with everyone in it freezing to attention.

"Won't you have my seat, sir?" a private or a sergeant would ask.

"No, son," General Bradley would reply, swinging on to the

181

running board and giving the boy a pat on the shoulder. "No, thank you, son. You're much more tired than I am. I just wanted to see how things are getting along here. Go ahead."

For five minutes or so he would remain, standing on the running board, finding out what he wanted to know before swinging down off the jeep, investigating an outpost, and hitchhiking his way on the next vehicle to come along.

The soldiers liked him for his American approach to authority and to war. They liked him enormously. Once, when he had gone ahead in a jeep and some of us were following him in a reconnaissance car, we got separated from him. Every time we passed an MP, we asked if he had seen General Bradley. Every MP's reply took one of two forms but was the same tribute. Either they would say, smiling proudly, "Yes, he's just passed this way." Or, looking glum, "Not today"; then with a sudden smile, "But we saw him yesterday."

Whether we could keep up with General Bradley or whether we hitchhiked or walked on our own, we saw much on our visits to both American beaches on those three days when he took us ashore.

Early each evening on the *Augusta,* before our sleepless nights began, we would get reports of the British advances around Bayeux or Caen; of our own lines as they deepened on both beaches; of the gradual consolidation of our two beachheads around the estuary; and later of the fierce fighting near Carentan. But by day, though Hanson Baldwin kept track of the higher strategy for us with the fine eye and knowledge of a professional, most of us—Jack Jarrell, Jack Rice, George Wheeler, Lieutenant Commander Griggs, Charles E. Thomas, Pho. M.1/c, with his eternal cameras, or young Captain Schlessinger of the Marines— wandered at will, not only surveying the cocoon of conquest but looking upon the Medusa's head of war. Our days ashore were ceaseless demonstrations of how different the impersonal battle maps are from the individual men and incidents, their real cartographers.

We saw the big German gun emplacements, sheltered from our

Beach Conference

Admiral Kirk, Admiral Hall, and General Bradley

Air Force by their ten-foot roofs of cement, where the Navy guns had scored their silencing hits. We saw enemy pillboxes scattered through the hills facing the beaches, pillboxes from which machine guns had taken a heavy toll of our men during the initial landing. We trudged down roads where the fields on either side were lined with stone walls or hedges against which the Germans with only moderate consideration had left signs reading, *"Achtung, Minen!"* We traveled through a countryside, blotched and bruised by war, but still green and lovely, old and meticulously cultivated. The countryside had that outraged look of a wounded neutral, which is always nature's wartime look when it is victimized by the foolishness and brutality of men. The meadows and the vegetation were different from those just across the Channel. The foliage and the agriculture were somehow coarser, rougher. The fields, though combed and rolled for centuries, appeared to have been finished with fluffy paintbrush rather than with that pencil which Emerson contended had replaced the plow in England.

In our hitchhiking or our walking we talked to countless soldiers—privates, sergeants, corporals, young officers—all of them dusty, sweaty, and in good spirits. They cheerfully admitted they had had a hard time at first; only they told us so in stronger language.

We passed house after house with its walls punctured or destroyed. We saw two gnarled old people, a man and woman, models for Millet, poking in the ruins of what three days before had been their home, seeking to retrieve all that remained of their possessions and carry them off in a baby carriage.

We saw a few blown bridges, small ones, and some tanks abandoned at the roadside. Our Army Engineers had already replaced these old stone bridges with structures of their own. The fact that more bridges were not blown may have indicated the speed of the Germans' retreat. We saw the widespread, glistening wings of some gliders that had been happy in their landings and the wreckage, in fields spiked with posts, of others that most decidedly had not.

184

Looking Seaward

We passed meadows with cows grazing in them, the whole scene so idyllic that we questioned the Invasion's reality. On the first Sunday, with our faces coated, our eyes smarting from the dust raised by the never-ending procession of our guns and vehicles, we passed through a village, hardly visible. Yet at the side of the street in this war-created Dust Bowl, we saw a little French girl, her curls as neatly ordered and her pink dress as chic as if on a peaceful Sabbath she were strolling to the Madeleine.

We visited a headquarters near the front in one area where officers, grim, unshaven and intent, were poring over maps. On a grassy hill near by we saw the disemboweled body of a young American, his arms spread, his head sunk to one side. His body was kept there as a warning to save others from paying his price for having been so unwise as to walk, in spite of orders, across lands not yet cleared of mines.

We entered the courtyards of old Norman farmhouses, their roofs tattered in places and their resistant stone walls downed here or there. Alongside old wagons we found our jeeps as orderly in their placing as cars serving a headquarters should be; while in front of them geese conducted their undisturbed parades, and all around them the centuries waged a conflict of their own.

We saw stunned peasants standing in little groups on sidewalks rough with rubble and glass. Some of these peasants waved. Many did not. Quite naturally, they were dazed by what had happened to their villages. Their interest was the number of their friends or families killed or wounded; their concern was what was left of those belongings it had taken them lifetimes of hard labor to acquire. Were they apathetic? Were they undemonstrative because in France they represent the temperamental equivalents of our New England farmers? Rot. They had been bludgeoned by war. They were still reeling from its blows. They were confused. Liberators who must destroy in order to liberate are confusing. It must be difficult, even in the interest of nice news stories, to cheer men who in the cause of freedom—your freedom and their own—have just been compelled to flatten your home or kill your brother.

Pastoral

Norman Conquest

The children waved more than the old people. They asked for gum and often got it. Our soldiers were friendliness itself. They waved and waved. And smiled good-naturedly. And called *"Bon jour"* and *"Vive la France"* in accents new to the Academy. One small boy of about eight, responding to our Army's salutations from the roadside, made clear in a single gesture how confusing these past and present happenings were to all Norman youngsters. For four years, in other words for half his life, this boy had lived under German occupation. Now, overnight, France was free; and so was he. With the best of good intentions, he returned our soldiers' waves with one of the most eloquent, the most revelatory compromises ever achieved in pantomime. First, with great solemnity, he raised his right arm skyward in a manner guaranteed to win the *Führer's* approval. Then, no less earnestly, the small fingers on his right hand spread to form Mr. Churchill's famous V for Victory. Events had moved too swiftly for him.

Along the shoulders of the roads and in the fields we sometimes saw soldiers raking the ground with mine detectors. The crop for which they gardened scientifically was death scientifically planted. They and their harvest were symbols of the double life lived by modern science; expressions of its positive and negative genius; of its coexistent strivings to cure or kill.

We stopped one day by General Collins's temporary headquarters. No setting could have been more Hollywood-French than this one now serving as a center for the grim business of war. A gray plaster building pretending to be a château; a courtyard and a stable, modern though striving to look old; an artificial mill pond; even a huge, flowering horse chestnut. At least the horse chestnut was real, in a background more photogenic than authentic. It was as real as the American soldiers everywhere visible. Like them it cast real shadows, too.

At General Collins's headquarters, incidentally, we saw two GI's bring in a frightened Nazi in green-gray. He was a uniformed sniper, left behind the retreating German lines to operate alone. Both of his shaking hands were held above his head. In one he carried ridiculously a little Nazi flag as though that would be

Nazi Sniper Brought In

a sure way of winning friends and influencing people.

Snipers were plentiful and costly. Once, immediately ahead of us, we saw an American soldier belly his way out of the bushes at one side of the road, his rifle aimed. He waved us down. A platoon followed him crawling across the road in the same fashion to seek the shelter of the stone wall lining the field beyond, in which there was a sniper.

Two other platoons closed in on this same sniper from hedges at either side of the field. They closed in on him as stealthily, as relentlessly, as ever the Federal troops surrounded John Wilkes Booth in the tobacco barn. There was a pause which only a stop watch could clock. Then the crackle of their rifle fire was heard.

Snipers were so numerous that every movie-trained son of America wanted to believe the stories about beautiful lady snipers, French girls dressed as men, who expressed their affection for their departed German lovers by reaching for a gun and taking pot shots at Americans. Romance is a form of marijuana men find hard to forswear. No doubt, the closer the ugly reality the greater their need to inhale it.

In the midst of destruction, in villages at first glance blasted and empty, it amazed—and reassured—us to see how quickly, how doggedly, life reasserts itself. The life force is as strong in men as it is in ants—which is fortunate, since in wartime men and their villages are held as expendable as ants and their hills.

Timidly men, women, and children would reappear, blinking at what they saw, dazed by what they had undergone. Then they would set about excavating their new lives from the ruins of the old, piecing together bits of the lost pattern, continuing as best they could to do what they had done, and searching for the means to do it. Some of them, impassive and indestructible, continued to live in their own worlds, scarcely noticing the traffic which choked their streets and roads or the new military world which engulfed them.

Seeing them, all I could think of was those peasants I had seen on the rim of the hill facing Cassino the day after the monastery had been bombed. Both the German batteries and our own were

191

blackening the sky with a heavy barrage. Yet I remembered passing in the midst of the battle a partially destroyed Italian farmhouse, behind the remains of which an American gun crew was
stooping for protection as it fired. Although the war was in truth
in their backyard, the peasant owners of this farmhouse ignored
it. Oblivious to its dangers, they went about their business, un-
helmeted and unarmed; the old women bending over a near-by
brook to do their washing and to gossip, some young children
laughing under a tree while milking their goats. In Normandy
we encountered many times the same odd themes of life and
death, of peace and war, played contrapuntally.

We could not help noticing as we drove through the villages,
or passed farmhouses that had been hit, or looked at the toppled
steeples of churches where the Germans had placed machine-gun
nests, how mortal are the wounds man can inflict on what man
has built, and how picayune are the scars left upon the landscape
by man's biggest guns or bombs.

From the beaches, especially from the bluffs on Admiral Hall's
beach, our sea strength was even more impressive than when seen
at sea. We could then appreciate its full panoramic spread and
look out to a more distant horizon. Even then, what we could see
was no more than a fraction of it. We envied our fliers their view.

The men pouring in from these ships, the equipment snailing
shoreward on rhino ferries, and the LST's with their jaws open on
the sands, we watched with fascination from the hills. We could
follow these forces inland, as the trucks and guns and tanks rolled
down the roads, flanked on either side by GI's. Anyone could
comprehend these features of the design. They were as obvious
as the simple fact that in war the final job is done by the impact
of the bayonet of the infantry on the belly of the enemy.

But once in the interior, once the great design broke up into
small single units, facing unpredictable hazards and subject to
sudden successes or reverses in this meadow or that village square,
we became confused. In spite of field telephones and communication wires which festooned the trees, we could not understand
how anyone ever kept track of all these forces, and their supplies,

Casualties

moving forward as if they knew where they were going. We could ·
not grasp this ordered chaos. At least we now understood why,
for such exasperating intervals, there were gaps in the lines on
the wall maps in our Joint Operations hut. The wonder was these
were ever filled in.

Whenever we thumbed a ride in a jeep or a DUKW, as the
long lines of our mechanized strength drove through the rem-
nants of a French village—St. Laurent-sur-Mer, Vierville, Isigny,
it did not matter which—some of us experienced, however illogi-
cally, that uncomfortable feeling, which conquerors must enjoy,
of having forced our way into someone else's house.

Although the mere suggestion of the conqueror's role embarrassed us so far as France was concerned, we were genuinely happy
whenever we saw Germans prisoners. The Nazis were the enemy.
Their presence in France explained ours. What distressed us was
what we had had to do to France and the French in order to rid
them of their conquerors. This only increased our dislike of the
Nazis.

We saw four groups of Nazi prisoners on our first day ashore.
One of these was near the water's edge, just behind the barbed
wire, now neatly pierced, which these Nazis had once thought
added to their invulnerability. Two other groups of some two
hundred each we came across in bull pens further inland. The
fourth group consisted of three German hospital corpsmen. They
were sitting on the ground, under guard, in a field hospital,
watching with no show of interest a young American soldier, with
a bandaged, blood-stained head, die on a stretcher. His face was
just being covered by his Army blanket when we came up. All
around him were other dead or wounded young Americans or
Britishers.

We were to see many more German prisoners on our next two
days ashore. We were to see them being marched to the bull pens
in great numbers, to see columns of them walking out across the
beaches as our own men streamed in. We were to see them sitting
sullen or silent behind barbed wire; laughing as they gobbled up
K-rations or smoked cigarettes; digging latrines at the field hos-

Master Race

Wounded German Hospital-Bound

pitals; carrying their own wounded or ours; digging graves for our dead or theirs. We were to see one captured Lieutenant Colonel, a surgeon, reequipped by our doctors, working with his own corpsmen and taking excellent care of German casualties.

For the most part, these Nazis were thin, scrubby, and sorry examples of the Super Race. They bore no resemblance to the fine physical specimens we had brought back from Sicily and Africa. They were a mixed lot, too; strange sandwich men for their master's theory of racial purity. They were Czechs, Poles, Yugoslavs, no less than Germans. One group was even Mongolian, claiming to be from Turkestan but at first glance easily mistaken for Japanese.

Many of the Germans were boys of sixteen or seventeen. Invariably, if they could muster any broken English or when spoken to through interpreters, these youngsters were the ones who still championed Hitler, who still could not understand what had happened to them, who still expected a German victory. They made one wonder about the future. No armistice, no peace treaty would set them right. Their minds had been captives since childhood. Being prisoners was to them no new experience. Hitler had seen to that. The older men were different. They had had enough. They were glad the war was over for them.

To come face to face with captured Nazis is an odd experience. Before Tamerlane and ever since, men have doubtless surveyed prisoners through strange eyes. They dislocate the normal vision. They are so many men all at one time. The fact that prisoners are men, like their captors, only complicates the judgment and adds to the disesteem in which they are held.

Men they are, men in deep trouble, men broken and denied the source of their pride and strength; but they are the enemy, too. In the case of these Nazis not only had their guns been pointing in different directions from our own; their minds had been no less opposed. This is what placed them in a category far removed from those who, having taken their final chances in the lottery of war, just happen to have lost. It was hard to have the normal respect for losers who were lost before they began. The

197

guilt of their masters was on these men. They could not escape their share in the horrors they had permitted to occur.

These prisoners were different not because they belonged to a different race. Race creates no barriers between men whose spirits speak the same language, whose eyes are fastened on the same goal, whose hearts share the same hopes. These men were different in their approach to life, perhaps even to death. Each one of them was a small embodiment of the reasons for the world's agony.

We saw them through insurmountable barricades of belief, through the eyes of their propaganda no less than our own. Which propaganda was the more damaging it was hard to say. We saw them remembering not only their past and our present, but considering our future. We saw them with hatred tempered by contempt, and contempt diluted by a kind of side-show curiosity.

We looked at them with wonder that men could be so, could believe what they must believe. We were aware that they, like us, were only doing what they felt it was their duty to do. Yet we were appalled that men could have made a duty of murder, pillage, terror, injustice, race slavery, and darkness. We knew that the army of which they had been a part had, among professional armies, been one of the finest. But we were compelled to judge that army in terms of the state it had been willing to serve. We held these prisoners both dangerous and despicable for having consented to function as so much as commas in the living edition of *Mein Kampf*.

We also knew, however, that these men who were the enemy were now the enemy stripped of his pretensions. They were the enemy trapped and taken, removed from the field. Because of this, each one of them was reassuring. Each one meant that the myth of supremacy to which he had subscribed was a lie. Each one was a guarantee that—to his small extent—the horror was abating. Even so, they were pitiable as men because they were defeated; left dreamless, helpless, and, we hoped, disillusioned. Enough of our own men were prisoners in Germany to make us

Nach England at Last

German Prisoners Outward Bound

Racial Purity

realize how these men must feel and how we would feel were the situation reversed.

But to look at them, and to think of the Germany which Madame de Staël discovered a little more than a century ago for a France suffering then not from being conquered but from a conqueror of her own, was to despise them the more. They had betrayed not only our present but their past.

We searched their faces in vain for any justification of their claims to superiority. The faces of these captured *Herrenvolk* revealed only ignorance, stupidity, and fatigue. Were they good or evil as individuals? Judging them under such circumstances, in haste, in the midst of war, from one uniform to another, we could not pretend to know this with any fairness. We wondered how as a group we appeared to them, and would have given more than a penny for their thoughts. Again there was no way of knowing. In spite of the appeals they made to our weak-minded sympathy, they explained why a dog barks when he sees a cat. The breed was different. That was all.

No one could have remained untouched by the field and evacuation hospitals or by the gallantry shown there by the doctors and corpsmen no less than by the wounded. We visited several of these hospitals, led to them by the red crosses on the tops of their brown tents and the shell-scarred ambulances which kept heading back to them, rolling down those same roads on which young Americans by the thousands were streaming to the front to form that two-way traffic which is war.

Off the main road, a village of tents would emerge above the hedges; a corner of salvation; movable; ready to follow the lines forward, though functioning as if it had been there always and always planned to remain in just this place. Turning into this village, past bushes floured with dust, we would come upon ambulances being unloaded. And upon row after row of litters which, when sorted, had been placed in various sections according to the seriousness of the cases, with our wounded here, the German wounded there, often with wounded civilians being cared for, too.

There were civilians—white-haired old women, dressed in black, with faces of ivory; middle-aged men in smocklike coats; and little children. Modern warfare distributes its pains impartially. It makes no distinctions between those in and out of uniform. It tolerates no immunities. Its eagerness to wound is total.

One morning at a field hospital we looked up to see a horse come through the entrance, pulling the kind of cart that was a tumbrel in the bloody days of the Revolution. It was precisely the kind of cart that David saw when he sketched the Widow Capet being taken to the guillotine. A peasant woman, tired, bespectacled, and scared, was driving. She was bringing a strange produce to a strange market. Loaded on sacks at the bottom of the cart were four little girls, their eyes swollen and damaged, their faces bloody and encircled with rags. We were told that they had been playing too near to enemy booby traps or hand grenades.

The hush of city hospitals was on these emergency wards, even under the open sky. Only the mildly wounded talked. With their arms in slings or their heads bandaged, they talked about their home towns; about Brooklyn, dear old Brooklyn and the Dodgers, about 42nd Street at night, about Detroit, Waco, or Champlain.

The paratroopers in particular had stirring tales to tell of tumbling earthward at 1:45 on the morning of D-day, near the town of Beaumont, and landing in the black swamp waters of those pastures which the Germans had flooded behind the beaches in Admiral Moon's area. Some had been shot at by machine guns before they could do the shooting themselves; then mortars had turned on them. Yet many had escaped lightly. These laughed when they thought of their good fortune. It is something to have survived; just to be alive after having come so close to death. They laughed until they remembered Jack or Jim who had not been so lucky. Then the lines of their faces would fall. Then they would do the only thing they could do—shake their heads.

The seriously wounded, and those suffering from lesser wounds, waited in silence under their brown blankets. Either with pained eyes rolled partially back they stared straight above them, or they

202

Total War

kept their eyes closed tight and pressed their teeth against their lower lips. And waited. They were waiting their turn for plasma, for fresh dressings, or for the operating tables in the central tents.

Funny things—those central tents, so hot in the sun. When first we entered them, they made us think of the tents used for side shows in small circuses at home. The same smell of parched and trampled grass underfoot; the same scent of sun-drenched canvas.

Soon, however, rows of litters became discernible in the darkness. They were long rows, stretching far on either side of the sunlit entrances into a mist of shadows. Before we had left these tents, what originally, in the horror of first impressions, had struck us as a menagerie of pain seemed a miracle of mercy.

These doctors and these corpsmen were working unstintingly, on twenty-four-hour shifts if need be. They were writing down case histories on the labels attached to each patient. They were washing these dusty, bleeding men. They were feeding them, giving them blood transfusions, administering sulpha or penicillin. Or, under the glaring lights in the long operating tents, where two operations were in progress at the same time, they were performing, as spotlessly in white as if they were in any good hospital back home, surgical feats of every variety and difficulty.

Whatever could be done to undo what had been done a few miles away by the destructive sciences of battle they were doing. Their function was life; the gunners', death. They were positives in a world of negatives. Even in the inferno of war, they must have wondered by what mischance Hippocrates had become confused with Sisyphus. They were matching their skills against the skills of the gunmakers, the shrapnel manufacturers, the grenade producers. More frequently by far than one might have believed possible, they were winning. Their victories were against death itself.

But guns have their labors to perform no less than doctors. They also speak for science, and no doctors can prevent them from doing their wartime duty. At the water's edge and in the countryside back of both beaches, Madame Tussaud had spread her waxen horrors out of doors.

204

Lt. (j.g.) Mitchell Jamieson

The Wounded

Resting

Emergency Ward

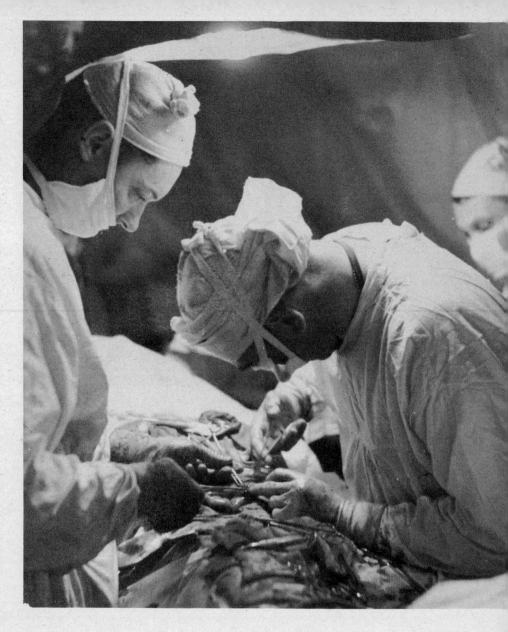

Surgeons at War

In fields inland or crumpled under dusty bushes at the road-side, we saw many of our young dead; many German dead, too, the latter often with their faces the gray-green of their uniforms. Many of our dead were the victims of snipers. Sometimes the blood had already rusted their pale cheeks. Sometimes on their temples it was still as shiny and bright as wine-red lacquer. Always these boys clutched at the earth, with their yellowed nails black at the tips. Almost always, in spite of mutilations or the frozen agony of their bodies, their faces were so strangely relaxed that one understood afresh why death is spoken of as a release.

To us who passed them each was not only a soldier unknown but an Unknown Soldier. Each stabbed the heart, though never again with quite the same sickening disquiet as did the first one we saw. It is melancholy to realize how quickly in war one grows accustomed to death. Not as a threat to the ill or the old, but as the lot of the healthy and the young. One is never hardened to it. Never entirely prepared to accept it. But ready to expect it as a commonplace; to admit it as what must be, hastened though it is in the coming; to know it will be there like the shadow on the sundial; to try to look upon it as a part of victory; to try to take it on war's own premises.

Of all the ways in which war overrides and ignores what is individual in men none is so hard to accept as the way in which, when it is too late, death re-creates an individual out of someone who has fallen singly from the ranks. In his loneliness by a foreign roadside, this man or that ceases to be Government Issue, a mass commodity produced by a mass response out of a mass need and hope. He once again becomes man's issue, and woman's too. He is one life cut short and scarcely tasted; with something of that life written on the mask which is now his face; with more written there than the form telegram can hope to express which will leave his family disconsolate, with a sorrow beyond remedy, and the world how much the poorer no one will ever know.

Men appear to become smaller in death. Their bodies shrink when denied the spirits they once housed. Their uniforms hang loose, styleless, disheveled, as if suddenly a size too large, as if

Sieg Heil!

they had found new owners. When these men were gathered up for burial, when their blankets covered their faces, what remained of their living had likewise dwindled. The little batch of blood-stained letters from home, the wrinkled snapshots, the unfinished package of cigarettes, the chewing gum, the stale half-eaten chocolate bar, the bits of string, the jackknife, and the overseas edition of a book—these were all that now spoke for the hungers they had once known and for lives which had reached out to touch other lives. These possessions were the more poignant because of the resemblance they bore to the ill-assorted but eloquent trophies to be found in any young boy's pockets.

We saw these men when they had fallen singly. We also saw them when some four hundred of them, soldiers and sailors, and about two hundred Germans were stretched on the ground awaiting burial. The cemetery in which prisoners had dug the graves was a meadow, high on a hilltop overlooking the beach on which many of these boys had died. Out to sea our ships darkened the blue water.

In this quiet meadow, where less than a week ago the enemy had felt impregnable, these young men had again surrendered their individuality. They were too numerous, too anonymous, too commonplace to be granted that concentration of affection suffered in the flower-banked funerals of those we love at home. Yet they disturbed the heart. Also the mind.

They were now parts of a force once more; fragments of the Invasion; reminders of how costly so precious a thing as liberty must be. They were covered with canvas which shone white in the sun. Only a clutched hand emerged here or there. Or a tuft of hair, stiff with dust or dandruff.

The smell of death was heavily upon this meadow. We, inhaling it, thought of Ernest Hemingway's description. The smell haunted our nostrils. It was sickly sweet, and over-sweetly sick, as if a gardenia had been dipped in vomit. In spite of the fresh breeze blowing in off the Channel, it made us, out of doors, long to open a window. It, too, was part of war; very much a part.

But even in war death cannot keep pace with life. At least for

Death Wholesale

long. The beaches below us were teeming with new arrivals; the landing craft and LST's were pouring in; the transports continuing to empty. When we left the cemetery, the smell of death still with us, and came back to the main road, this road had never before seemed so crowded or alive. Vehicles and men without number were surging up it.

They were far too numerous to be counted as replacements. Trucks, guns, jeeps, supplies, ambulances, and great columns of trudging infantry were overrunning the countryside. In her soda jerkers and mechanics, her clerks and laborers, her teachers and farmers, America had found a harvest of armed men to make ridiculous Jason's military seedlings. The Americans who marched or rode were dusty, young, alert, and strong; the life force in full tide and in khaki.

The men and materials America had moved to Britain across a perilous Atlantic had been moved again, this time to the Continent and in spite of greater dangers. The plans, so long made, so minute in detail, so grandiose in scale, so hazardous in execution, had become history. One trembled to think of what would have happened had they miscarried. The Invasion, however, was now securely launched. Our beachheads were established. We were streaming ashore, even as a few miles to the east of us the Canadians and British were pouring in. The mass migration was once again on the move, this time augmented; indeed, doubled in its size and strength by our Allies.

We knew by our last day ashore that our Invasion was a conquest; our conquest a liberation. It was then that in front of or over numerous buildings we saw the tricolor flying. At the outset, these flags had reappeared slowly. Now in the villages and over farmhouses there were many of them. Among all the spring flowers none was so welcome that year.

From a purely material point of view a flag may be no more than a strip of bunting, discolored by the dyes of a nation's tastes. No material, however, is stout enough or large enough to hold what a flag holds. Its pigmentation is not limited to the obvious reds or whites or blues one sees on it. It is colored by a nation's

213

Happy Landing for a Glider

history and a people's hopes. It is at once a reminder of what has been faced in common and a gesture to advance. To those living under it, which means living by it, a flag expresses what no amount of words can hope to say. In a world scientific and materialistic, and supposedly rational, it still speaks as a symbol, proud, coalescing, mystical.

The tricolor was for us the most reassuring of symbols. It meant more than that a strip of France was now made free, hence French, again. It meant that the whole of France could now be freed, that other flags would in time fly unthreatened where the swastika had flown. This meant that the long, dark agony was approaching its end in Europe; its reason justified, its meaning made the clearer.

When we returned to the *Augusta* that night, we learned that General Bradley had moved his headquarters ashore before luncheon. This was D plus four. The two beaches had by then been joined. The fighting had moved inland in most places in the Invasion area beyond the range of our guns. The first naval phase of the assault was over.

Much remained to be done. The Cherbourg batteries had to be neutralized. The flow of supplies and men across the Channel had to be maintained. Many weary miles still separated us from Paris, and more from Berlin. But in both the Eastern and Western Task Force areas the beginning had been made that would lead to peace.

We thought much about that peace, whether it could avert the next war. We thought, too, about war as we had this time encountered it. We thought about what it had taught us in democracy and sacrifice, and what it had offered us in comradeship, excitement, and experience. We thought about its waste and cruelty, its barbarisms which were the more barbarous because they were the practice of men pretending to be civilized. We thought about science and how it had had to be perverted into an agent of destruction; about a world which, having waited too long, had been compelled to save itself by pouring its resources into fireworks, and squandering its time, its talents, its energies, and its

215

The Life Force in Khaki

youth on scientific murder. We thought about the living no less than the dead. About the fatigue which will follow the peace as the enemy's last and most formidable division. About the danger of men expecting or hoping, however naturally, to withdraw again to the kind of living which had made all this necessary. We also thought about the high courage exacted by war.

Courage we had seen everywhere. Men dying gallantly, or facing death cheerfully, for what they felt but could not phrase. Without subtracting one iota from that courage or the admiration due it, we wondered about the emphasis in our thinking which so glorifies the mere act of dying.

Everywhere the patriotic emphasis is on the gallant death for one's country, rather than the gallant life. The worship of the hero's death is a romantic flourish oddly out of place in the credo of an age priding itself on its realism. Men who find the pattern for it in the Crucifixion apparently forget that this death was the last, not the first, of the glories of the life which preceded it. The esteem in which we hold the hero's death, stressing it even more than we do his life, is an odd survival. It is a medievalism which insists that this world is a poor threshold to the next and that we exist here only to live there.

Men stand in proper awe of death because of its finality. Their fear of it is the fear of the unknown. For those willing to embrace it for an idea, they have the respect such high and selfless courage merits. But they forget that the known, which is modern warfare, holds terrors the unknown cannot exceed.

Unquestionably men lose their manhood when they are not willing to die for the belief which is their country. Yet no less unquestionably they also lose that manhood by their dying. They lose their usefulness, too. The mere dying, though magnificent, ought not to be enough. The living for one's country should count for more.

Such is our fetish of the gallant death that we forgive the Charleses of this earth because we believe they have redeemed their foolish lives by ten manly minutes on the scaffold. We respect our heroes more for their willingness to die than for their

217

ability to live. Yet if ever there is to be a peace which is not an armistice, men must learn to live at least as well as they now know how to die. Because the mischance of death in action is the price of war, and active living should be the responsibility of peace.

Perhaps in our self-questionings we were asking for too much. Perhaps we should have been satisfied with a mammoth Invasion, brilliantly planned and triumphantly executed, and the hopes of freedom and peace which it had everywhere raised. But it is impossible for rational men to be satisfied with war, thankful as they must be to have the side of freedom win.

If only men could learn to act in time. If only men could realize that the maintenance of a proud peace requires more vigilance than the prosecution of a just war. Yes, and equal courage. And greater character and characters. If only, among all the things this war has taught us, we have gained sufficient wisdom to make another war unnecessary and unthinkable. Because the last people on earth who want a war are the men in their right senses who must fight it.

Acknowledgments

All but two of the illustrations in this book are the work of U. S. Navy men. The cover is by Lieutenant Dwight Shepler, USNR, as are several other sketches. He and Lieutenant (j.g.) Mitchell Jamieson, USNR, are U. S. Navy Combat Artists. Other sketches are by Lieutenant William A. Bostick, USNR, and Alexander P. Russo, Sp. (p.) 2/c. Most of the English photographs were taken by the U. S. Navy Combat Photo Units Lieutenant Fred Garretson, USNR, and Lieutenant Lawrence Crolius, USNR; and almost all of the Invasion photographs were taken by Charles E. Thomas, Pho. M.1/c, USNR, who was on the *Augusta* and went into the beaches. My warm thanks are also due to Lieutenant Commander Barry Bingham, USNR, Lieutenant Commander Gregory Williamson, USNR, Lieutenant Arthur Newmyer, USNR, Lieutenant J. Richard Poisson, USNR, Lieutenant Peter J. Braal, USNR, and the Public Relations Staff in London, with whom I had the pleasure of working during the exciting days when the Invasion was being planned.